# Humor
# for Preaching
# and Teaching

Also by Edward K. Rowell

Fresh Illustrations for Preaching and Teaching
Quotes and Idea Starters for Preaching and
    Teaching

# Humor
# for Preaching
# and Teaching

*From Leadership Journal
and Christian Reader*

**Edward K. Rowell
and Bonne L. Steffen**

**Baker Books**

A Division of Baker Book House Co
Grand Rapids, Michigan 49516

Copublished by Christianity Today, Inc., and Baker Books
a division of Baker Book House Company
P.O. Box 6287, Grand Rapids, MI 49516-6287

Paperback edition published 1998

Printed in the United States of America

**Library of Congress Cataloging-in-Publication Data**

Humor for preaching and teaching : from leadership journal and Christian reader / Edward K. Rowell and Bonne L. Steffen, editors.
     p.    cm.
  Includes index.
  ISBN 0-8010-9025-3 (cloth)
  ISBN 0-8010-9065-2 (paper)
  1. Homiletical illustrations. 2. Anecdotes. I. Rowell, Edward K.
II. Steffen, Bonne L. III. Leadership journal. IV. Christian reader.
BV4235.H85H85   1996
251'.08—dc20                  96-30356

For information about academic books, resources for Christian leaders, and all new releases available from Baker Book House, visit our web site:
               http://www.bakerbooks.com

# Introduction

People think I'm funny. The problem is, they never think I'm funny when I think I'm funny.

Several years ago, I turned to walk through the glass doors at church and smacked into one of the full-length windows instead. As I staggered around the foyer, dazed and confused, everyone, including my wife, just howled. In fact, they still laugh about it. Some people are just sick.

Another time, I was officiating at a wedding in a historic church. As I made my grand entry from the little room behind the platform, the entire door and door frame came off in my hand. I turned to the groom for advice, but he already had that deer-in-the-headlights look. I searched the congregation for help, but they busted up laughing. So I laid the door next to the organ and took my place. Everyone (except the bride and her mother) said it was the most memorable wedding they'd ever attended.

As a result, I hate doors; and there are no door jokes in *Humor for Preaching and Teaching*. What you'll find instead are funny stories and one-liners, topically arranged and cross-referenced. We've even put together an index to help you locate the appropriate chuckle for the occasion.

From Abstinence to Zeal, you'll find just the right light-hearted illustration to freshen your message and drive home your point. Use them in your bulletin or newsletter. Better yet, buy hundreds of copies of this book for your church; then simply refer to the page number when you use one. Kind of like a humor hymnal.

*Humor for Preaching and Teaching* also contains some of our favorite cartoons from *Leadership* and *Christian Reader*. We've even included pastoral humor, for the next time you speak at the ministerial alliance or denominational meeting.

We're confident that *Humor for Preaching and Teaching* will become a valuable asset in your speaking and writing ministry. Not to mention that it will give you a grin.

If you want to inject some levity into your speaking, you can either use this great material, or invite me to speak in your place. Remember, though, I'm a lot harder on the facilities.

—Ed Rowell
Assistant Editor, LEADERSHIP
Carol Stream, Illinois

## Abstinence

I always scoffed at the idea of a generation gap—until recently, that is. While talking to my pre-teen daughter, I mentioned how important it was to be chaste.

"But why, Mom?" she asked. "I'd rather do the chasing myself instead of *being* chased."

—Janell Wheeler
*(Chastity, Purity)*

Dates used:_____

## Acceptance

Peter Marshall, former chaplain of the U.S. Senate, wrote a little poem worth recalling:

We have the nicest garbage man.
He empties out our garbage can.
He's just as nice as he can be.
He always stops and talks to me.
My mother doesn't like his smell.
But mother doesn't know him well.

—Calvin Miller
*(Assumptions, Prejudice)*

Dates used:_____

# Adultery

A third grade Sunday school teacher was uneasy about the lesson "Thou shalt not commit adultery." By way of introduction she asked, "Would someone please explain what adultery means?"

A young sage answered matter of factly, "Adultery is when a kid lies about his age."

—Jonathan R. Mutchler
*(Age, Ten Commandments)*

Dates used:_____

# Advent

Advent was one week away, so we thought we'd see what the children remembered from our family devotions the year before. "Who can tell me what the four candles in the Advent wreath represent?" I asked.

Luke jumped in with seven-year-old wisdom and exuberance. "There's love, joy, peace, and ... and ..."

"I know!" six-year-old Elise interrupted to finish her brother's sentence: "Peace and quiet!"

—Michelle L. Hardie
*(Christmas, Peace)*

Dates used:_____

# Afflictions

A hand-lettered sign nailed to a telephone pole said, "Lost dog with three legs, blind in left eye, missing right ear, tail broken, and recently castrated. Answers to the name of Lucky."

—Barbara Johnson
*(Attitude, Trouble)*

Dates used:_____

An insurance agent was writing a policy for a cowboy. "Have you ever had any accidents?" the agent asked.

"No, not really," replied the cowboy. "A horse kicked in a few of my ribs once. I got bit a couple of times by a rattlesnake, but that's about it."

"Don't you call those accidents?" demanded the agent.

"Oh, no," came the answer, "they did that on purpose."

—Herb Miller & Douglas Moore
*300 Seed Thoughts: Illustrative Stories for Speakers*
*(Accidents, Anxiety)*

Dates used:_____

You know it's going to be a bad day when:
You wake up in a hospital in traction, and your insurance agent tells you, "Your accident policy covers falling off the roof, but not hitting the ground." —Adapted from *Have a Good Day*
*(Anxiety, Stress)*

Dates used:_____


After Hurricane Andrew devastated south Florida, Patricia Christy was waiting in line for food. She vowed she was going to get out of that state. She was going to leave on the first plane out. She was determined to get as far away from the horror of hurricane damage as she possibly could and have a restful vacation.

I have just heard from Patricia Christy. She was standing in line for fresh water on the Hawaiian island of Kauai, having just gone through Hurricane Iniki!

—"Paul Harvey News"
*(Stress, Trouble)*

Dates used:_____

# Aging

Jeanne Calment, at 120 years and counting, is the oldest living human whose birth date can be authenticated. Recently she was asked to describe her vision for the future.

She replied, "Very brief."

—Clark Cothern
*(Attitude, Sense of Humor)*

Dates used:_____

A woman was interviewed by reporters on her 102nd birthday. When asked about the benefits of living past the century mark, she answered, "No peer pressure!"

—Win Arn
*(Peer Pressure, Sense of Humor)*

Dates used:_____

John Fetterman, rector of Grace Episcopal Church in Madison, Wisconsin, told of an elderly woman who died. Having never married, she requested no male pallbearers. In her handwritten instructions for her memorial service, she wrote, "They wouldn't take me out while I was alive; I don't want them to take me out when I'm dead." —*Homiletics* *(Funerals, Single Adults)*

Dates used:_____

A group of senior citizens were lounging on the patio of their retirement community. One looked up as a large flock of birds flew overhead. He nudged a companion who had dozed off. "Frank, you'd better move around a little bit. Those looked like buzzards closing in on us." *(Death, Laziness)*

Dates used:_____

# Appearances

When my great-niece was 5, she asked her grandmother, "Grandma, are you rotten on the inside?"

"No, sweetheart, why?" Grandma answered with some surprise.

"Because when apples are all wrinkled on the outside, they are rotten on the inside."

—Shermalee Ochoa
*(Aging, Character)*

Dates used:_____

## Assumptions

In *Point Man,* Steve Farrar tells this story:

The photographer for a national magazine was assigned to shoot a great forest fire. He was told that a small plane would be waiting to take him over the fire.

He arrived at the airstrip just an hour before sundown. Sure enough the Cessna was waiting. He jumped in with his equipment and shouted, "Let's go!" The pilot swung the plane into the wind and soon they were in the air.

"Fly over the north side of the fire," said the photographer, "and make several low-level passes."

"Why?" asked the nervous pilot.

"Because I'm going to take pictures!" retorted the photographer. "I'm a photographer, and photographers take pictures."

After a long pause, the pilot replied, "You mean, you're not the instructor?"

—Ron Willoughby
*(Danger, Fear)*

Dates used:_____

14

## Attitude

While watching the movie, *The Ten Commandments,* on television, four-year-old Melissa learned that one of God's names is "I Am That I Am." For days after, true to her contrary style, Melissa strode around the house pronouncing, "I'm not that I'm not!"

—Christie Kehn
*(Rebelllion, Ten Commandments)*

Dates used:_____

Way out West, a cowboy was driving down a road, his dog riding in back of the pickup truck, his faithful horse in the trailer behind. He failed to negotiate a curve and had a terrible accident.

Sometime later, a state police officer came upon the scene. An animal lover, he saw the horse first. Realizing the serious nature of its injuries, he drew his service revolver and put the animal out of it's misery. He walked around the accident and found the dog, also hurt critically. He couldn't bear to hear it whine in pain, so he ended the dog's suffering as well.

Finally he located the cowboy—who suffered multiple fractures—off in the weeds. "Hey, are you okay?" the cop asked.

The cowboy took one look at the smoking revolver in the trooper's hand and quickly replied, "Never felt better!"

*(Complaining, Mercy)*

Dates used:_____

# Authenticity

In *Becoming a Contagious Christian,* Bill Hybels and Mark Mittleberg tell this story:

A newly promoted colonel had moved into a makeshift office during the Gulf War. He was just getting unpacked when out of the corner of his eye, he noticed a private coming his way with a toolbox.

Wanting to seem important, he grabbed the phone. "Yes, General Schwarzkopf, I think that's an excellent plan." He continued, "You've got my support on it. Thanks for checking with me. Let's touch base again soon, Norm. Goodbye."

"And what can I do for you?" he asked the private.

"Ahhh, I'm just here to hook up your phone," came the rather sheepish reply.

—Ron Willoughby
*(Deceit, Pride)*

Dates used:_____

# Baptism

Although I was raised a Methodist, I became active in a Baptist church when I moved to a new community. One day I was helping a group of women clean the church kitchen after a social event. I emptied the large, electric coffee pot and handed it to the woman washing dishes.

"Can this be washed like everything else?" she asked.

"No," I replied. "This is a Methodist coffee pot. It says right here, Do NOT IMMERSE."

—Jane E. Vajnar
*(Denominations, Fellowship)*

Dates used:_____

As an adult Sunday school teacher, I'm often given fact sheets on new members so I can invite them to visit our class. While reading about one new member, I chuckled when I read under the "Circumstances of Salvation" this notation: "Accepted Christ in high school. Was baptized but would like to be reimbursed (crossed out) reimmersed."

—Steve Page
*(God's Gift, Salvation)*

Dates used:_____

A congregation installed a new baptistry in the sanctuary as part of an extensive remodeling project. But the county building inspector wouldn't okay its installation. "I can't," he said, "unless it has a separate septic tank."

The trustees couldn't understand why a septic tank would be needed for a baptistry. The building inspector saw their puzzled faces, so he explained, "It's to avoid pollution in the ground."

One of the church trustees finally said with a grin, "I guess it *would* pollute, with all those sins washed away!"

—Helen Daley
*(Sanctification, Sin)*

Dates used:_____

Our church had finally decided to invest in a P.A. system. As the technician and I made our way around the sanctuary we studied the best locations for the speakers. When we got to the front, the technician made a bee-line for the large opening in the front wall. He leaned over, practically disappearing. I could hear his question echoing from the baptistry, "What's a bathtub doing in a church?"

—Quincy Collins
*(Confusion, Perspective)*

Dates used:_____

# Beliefs

My daughter Barb and I were hired to conduct an in-depth survey. After a day of reading questions and writing responses, we were getting weary, but we decided to finish the last two people before calling it a day.

I dropped Barb at her final location and went to mine. I finished early, so I walked in on Barb just as she was finishing the personal data section, which included the question, "Religious Affiliation?"

I knew a hard day's work had finally gotten to Barb when I heard her ask, "And finally, what is your religious affliction?"

—Gusty Chartrand
*(Church, Faith)*

Dates used:_____

# Bible

It is truly astonishing what happens in Bible stories when they are retold by young scholars around the world. . .

God got tired of creating the world, so he took the Sabbath off. Adam and Eve were created from an apple tree. Noah's wife was called Joan of Ark. Lot's wife was a pillar of salt by day, but a ball of fire by night.

Samson was a strongman who let himself be led astray by a Jezebel like Delilah. Samson slayed the Philistines with the axe of the apostles.

Moses led the Hebrews to the Red Sea, where they made unleavened bread made without any ingredients. The Egyptians were all drowned in the desert. Afterwards, Moses went up on Mount Cyanide to get the Ten Amendments. The First Commandment was when Eve told Adam to eat the apple. The Fifth Commandment is to humor thy father and mother. The Seventh Commandment is thou shalt not admit adultery.

Moses died before he ever reached Canada. Then Joshua led the Hebrews in the Battle of Geritol. The greatest miracle in the Bible is when Joshua told his son to stand still and he obeyed him.

David was a Hebrew king skilled at playing

(continued)

the liar. He fought with the Finklesteins, a race of people who lived in biblical times. Solomon, one of David's sons, had 300 wives and 700 porcupines.

Jesus enunciated the Golden Rule, which says to do one to others before they do one to you. The people who followed the Lord were called the Twelve Decibels. The epistles were the wives of the apostles. One of the opossums was St. Matthew who was by profession a taximan.

St. Paul cavorted to Christianity. He preached holy acrimony, which is another name for marriage. A Christian should have only one wife. This is called monotony.

The things they teach in Sunday School these days!
—Roger Moberg
*(Inerrancy, Sunday School)*

Dates used:_____

# Blame

I went to my psychiatrist to be
psychoanalyzed,
   To find out why I killed the cat and
blackened my wife's eyes.
   He laid me on a downy couch to see
what he could find,
   And this is what he dregged up
from my subconscious mind.
   When I was one, my mommy locked
my dolly in the trunk,
   and so it follows naturally that I am
always drunk.
   When I was two, I saw my father kiss
the maid one day.
   That is why I suffer now from
kleptoman-e-ay.
   When I was three, I suffered from
ambivalence toward my brothers.
   That is just the reason why I poisoned
all my lovers.
   I'm so glad since I have learned that
lesson so well taught,
   That everything I do that's wrong is
someone else's fault.
                              —John Guest
                     *(Guilt, Responsibility)*

Dates used:_____

Two kids sat down for lunch. One opened his lunchbox and began to gripe. "Baloney again? This is the fourth day in a row! I'm sick and tired of baloney!"

His friend said, "I bet if you just tell your mom you don't like baloney, she'll fix you something else."

"Mom?" replied the first kid. "I fix my own lunches."

*(Complaining, Responsibility)*

Dates used:_____


At bedtime, Lillian Holcomb told her two grandsons a Bible story, then asked if they knew what the word *sin* meant. Seven-year-old Keith spoke up: "It's when you do something bad." Four-year-old Aaron's eyes widened. "I know a big sin Keith did today."

Annoyed, Keith turned to his little brother: "You take care of your sins, and I'll take care of mine."

—*Christian Reader*
*(Responsibility, Sin)*

Dates used:_____

A dog food company's newest product was not selling well. The president called in his management staff. "How's our advertising?" he asked.

"Great," replied the advertising executive. "This ad campaign will probably win the industry's top awards this year."

"All right," the president continued. "How about our product design?"

The production manager spoke up. "It's great, boss. Our new label and packaging scored high in every marketing test we ran."

"Hmmm. Well, how's our sales staff? Are they doing their job?"

The sales manager was quick to respond. "Oh, sure. Our people are the best in the business."

There was heavy silence as the president thought about what he'd just heard. "We've got great advertising, great packaging, a top-notch sales force, yet this product is coming in dead last in the dog food market. Does anyone have any idea what the problem might be?"

Everyone looked at each other. Finally, one brave soul spoke up. "It's those stupid dogs, sir. They just won't touch the stuff."

—John Maxwell, *Developing the Leader Within You*
*(Confusion, Responsibility)*

Dates used:_____

## Body of Christ

Carol, a clerk in our local Christian bookstore, often refers to a church as "the body." One week, a number of members of a local "body" had come to the bookstore to buy birthday gifts for their beloved pastor.

Later, that pastor, John, stopped at the store. He told Carol about the surprise party his congregation had given him the night before. Carol's heart was touched. Spontaneously, she exclaimed, "Oh, John, I just love your 'body'!"

The customers in the store burst into laughter, leaving a startled look on John's face—and Carol's, too.

—Martha E. Garrett
*(Church, Communication)*

Dates used:_____

## Budgets

The bad news: the average American has just $83.42 in the bank.

The good news: The average American is $4.6 trillion richer than the U.S. government.

—*The Hope Health Letter* (2/96)
*(Debt, Money)*

Dates used:_____

# Bureaucracy

New Chemical Discovered!

The heaviest element known to science was recently discovered by investigators at a major U.S. research university. The element, tentatively named *administratium,* has no protons or electrons and thus has an atomic weight of 0. However, it does have one neutron, 125 assistant neutrons, 75 vice neutrons and 111 assistant vice neutrons, giving it an atomic mass of 312. These 312 particles are held together by a force which involves a continuous exchange of meson-like particles called morons.

Since it has no electrons, *administratium* is inert. However, it can be detected chemically as it impedes every reaction it comes in contact with. According to its discoverers, just a minute amount of *administratium* can delay a one-second reaction to over four days.

*Administratium* has a normal half-life of approximately three years, at which time it does not decay, but instead undergoes a reorganization in which assistant neutrons, vice neutrons, and assistant vice neutrons exchange places. Some studies have shown that the atomic mass actually increases after reorganization.

—Unknown
*(Boards, Committees)*

Dates used:_____

# Christmas

It's time to recycle those leftover holiday fruitcakes. That's right. You can have your cake and use it, too.* Just consider the possibilities:

Pothole filler.

Shot put.

Speed bump.

Boat anchor.

Flower press.

Bed warmer (heat to 350 degrees).

Ice pack (chilled for 12 hours).

Chopping block.

Scratching post for your cat.

*User assumes all liability for busted toes, hernias, and other medical ailments resulting therefrom.

—Suzanne James, *America West Airlines Magazine*
*(Gifts, Recycling)*

Dates used:_____

# Church

Seen on a church sign:
WE CARE ABOUT YOU
Sundays 10 A.M. Only

—Gary Shank
*(Fellowship, Visitors)*

Dates used:_____

An oxymoron is an apparently self-contradictory expression like *jumbo shrimp, freezer burn,* and *working vacation.* A look around the church will uncover a few more expressions that fit the category.

Take, for example, when a pastor assures us that, due to Communion, he will be delivering a *mini sermon.*

Or the poster that announced the community Easter sunrise service would feature a *unified choir.* Whoever wrote that has obviously never sat in a choir loft.

Then there was the announcement in our bulletin noting that the church was looking for a *volunteer junior-high leader.* And the *short business meeting* announced by our board chairman to discuss hiring a *long-term youth pastor.*

Now that I've alerted you to their existence, you'll quickly find other Sunday morning oxymorons. But why take my word for it? I'm a *confirmed skeptic.*

—Eutychus in *Christianity Today*
*(Communication, Volunteers)*

Dates used:_____

# Church and State

It was the Sunday before Election Day, and our music department had just presented a skit about "The Publican and the Sinner." This was followed by prayer led by one of our senior members. In a resonant voice he prayed, "Lord, keep us from becoming like the Republicans we heard about this morning."

—Marlene Sims
*(Impact, Politics)*

Dates used:_____

## Cleverness

A man and his wife were checking out of a motel. They discovered the manager had charged them for a fresh basket of fruit put in the room every day. The man said, "How can you charge us for fresh fruit when we never ate any fruit from any basket on any day?"

The manager said, "It's not my fault you didn't eat it. It was there."

So this man took the bill and subtracted $150 from it. The manager said, "What in the world are you doing?"

The man said, "I am charging you $50 a day for kissing my wife."

The manager said, "I didn't kiss your wife."

The husband said, "That's not my fault. She was there."

—Larry Moyer
*(Bills, Expectations)*

Dates used:_____

# Comfort

It was one of the worst days of my life: the washing machine broke down, the telephone kept ringing, my head ached, and the mail carrier brought a bill I had no money to pay.

Almost to the breaking point, I lifted my one-year-old into his highchair, leaned my head against the tray, and began to cry.

Without a word, my son took his pacifier out of his mouth and stuck it in mine.

—Clara Null
*(Compassion, Sharing)*

Dates used:_____

## Commitment

Several years ago I visited a man who had stopped attending our church. Joe was getting up in years but was in fairly good health.

He greeted me at the door but hesitated to let me in. "Joe," I explained through the screen, "we've missed you in church. Is there any problem I should be aware of?"

"No," he replied. "I'm getting older and am having some trouble getting around. It's just too difficult for me to make church anymore."

"I'm sorry to hear that. There are a lot of steps here and at church. I know you don't have a car, and it's a good mile from here to church. Is there any way we can help?"

"I don't know who I'd ask for a ride," he said, and I detected the implication: *And I don't want you to arrange one, either.*

"How about if I visit you regularly as a shut-in, instead? I could come to your house each month with Communion and a tape recording of one of the services for you to listen to at your convenience. How would you like that?"

Joe's face dropped suddenly, and his eyes averted mine. "That wouldn't work out because I'm gone so much. You'd seldom find me at home."

—John E. Kassen
*(Excuses, Visitation)*

Dates used:_____

# Committees

George Will quipped, "Football combines the two worst things about American life. It is violence punctuated by committee meetings."

—Robert Byrne
*(Sports, Violence)*

Dates used:_____


An old legend says that when God created the world, the angels were in awe. As he created the animals, the angels asked to give it a try. God agreed, so the animal-creation committee designed the platypus, a creature with the bill of a duck, the fur of a dog, the tail of a beaver, and the feet of a frog.

Since that day, there have been no committees in heaven.

*(Confusion, Vision)*

Dates used:_____

—Jonny Hawkins
*(Boards, Procrastination)*

Dates used:_____

## Communication

Crystal, our five-year-old daughter, recently met an Amish girl her age. Within a few minutes they were off, hand-in-hand, to play. I caught glimpses of them chattering and giggling. Even though Sylvia, the Amish girl, spoke a Pennsylvania Dutch dialect, she and Crystal got along well.

Later I asked Crystal, "Could you understand anything Sylvia said to you?"

"No," she replied.

"But you played so nicely together. How?"

"Oh, Mommy. We understood each other's giggles."

—Bonnie Hellum Brechill
*(Harmony, Laughter)*

Dates used:_____

Four-year-old Jason was visiting his grandparents. Grandpa was in his study intently reading. Jason walked in carrying a peach, said something Grandpa didn't catch, and handed the peach to him.

Thinking his wife had sent him a snack, Grandpa took it and ate it. Just as he swallowed the last bite, Jason, with lip quivering, said, "But, Pap, I didn't want you to eat it. I just wanted you to get the worm out!"

—Sue Hammons
*(Help, Listening)*

Dates used:_____

*The Los Angeles Times* recently printed a sampling of signs from around the world that attempted to communicate in English.

In a hotel elevator in Paris: *"Please leave your values at the front desk."*

In a hotel in Zurich: *"Because of the impropriety of entertaining guests of the opposite sex in the bedroom, it is suggested that the lobby be used for this purpose."*

On the door of a Moscow inn: *"If this is your first visit to Russia, you are welcome to it."*

Announcement in a Russian newspaper: *"There will be a Moscow exhibition of arts by 15,000 Soviet Republic painters and sculptors. These were executed over the past two years."*

In a Bucharest hotel lobby: *"The lift is being fixed for the next day. During that time we regret that you will be unbearable."*

—B. Paul Greene
*(Evangelism, Misunderstanding)*

Dates used:_____

# Communion

When I was a child, our church celebrated the Lord's Supper every first Sunday of the month. At that service, the offering plates were passed twice: before the sermon for regular offerings, and just prior to Communion for benevolences. My family always gave to both, but they passed a dime to me only to put in the regular offering.

One Communion Sunday when I was nine, my mother, for the first time, gave me a dime for the benevolent offering also. A little later when the folks in our pew rose to go to the Communion rail, I got up also. "You can't take Communion yet," Mother told me.

"Why not?" I said. "I paid for it!"

—Paul Francisco
*(Expectations, Giving)*

Dates used:_____

My brother-in-law, who is a minister, responded to a Red Cross appeal for blood donations. When he didn't come home by the time his young son expected him, the boy asked his mother, "Is Dad going around visiting all the sick people?"

His mother replied, "He's giving blood."

"But we know it's really grape juice, don't we, Mom?"
—Priscilla Larson
*(Example, Sacrifice)*

Dates used:_____

Seth, our curious five-year-old, couldn't keep his eyes off us when we were taking Communion. A few seconds later, I stole a peek—he was watching his daddy at prayer after receiving the elements. "Good parental example," I thought.

My gratification was short-lived as Seth leaned over and whispered to me, "What's in that stuff? You eat it and go right to sleep."

—Sherri Yates
*(Example, Prayer)*

Dates used:_____

41

One weekend my little brother was visiting our grandparents in another town. They took him to church with them, and one Sunday after church, he asked what Communion was all about.

Granddad replied, "That was Jesus' last supper."

My little brother replied, "Boy, they didn't give him much, did they?"

—Elaine Borcher
*(Last Supper, Stinginess)*

Dates used:_____

## Community

A three-year-old girl listened intently to the children's sermon. The minister explained that God wants everyone to get along and love each other.

"God wants us all to be one," he said.

To which the little girl replied, "But I don't want to be one. I want to be four!"

—Marilyn McCoy
*(Age, Communication)*

Dates used:_____

# Compassion

The instructor from a dog training workshop in Salt Lake City noted that a dog's disposition can be tested by the owner. If the owner will fall down and pretend to be hurt, a dog with a bad temper will tend to bite him. But a good dog will show concern and may lick the fallen owner's face.

Susan Matice attended the class and then decided to test her two dogs. While eating pizza in her living room, she stood up, clutched her heart, screamed and fell to the floor. Her two dogs looked at her, looked at each other, then raced to the coffee table for her pizza.

—Associated Press (1-17-91)
*(Attitude, Greed)*

Dates used:_____

A man finally went to the doctor after weeks of symptoms. The doctor examined him carefully, then called the patient's wife into his office.

"Your husband is suffering from a very rare form of anemia. Without treatment, he'll be dead in a few weeks. The good news is it can be treated with proper nutrition.

"You will need to get up early every morning and fix your husband a hot breakfast—pancakes, bacon, and eggs. He'll need a big, home-cooked lunch every day and then an old-fashioned, meat-and-potatoes dinner every evening. It would be especially helpful if you could bake frequently—cakes, pies, homemade bread—these are the things that will allow your husband to live symptom-free.

"One more thing. His immune system is weak, so it's important that your home be kept spotless at all times. Do you have any questions?"

The wife had none.

"Do you want to break the news, or shall I?" asked the doctor.

"I will," the wife replied.

She walked into the examination room. The husband, sensing the seriousness of his illness, asked her, "It's bad, isn't it?" She nodded, tears welling up in her eyes. "Tell me, what is it?" he asked her.

*(continued)*

With a sob, the wife blurted out, "The doctor says you're gonna die!"

*(Dedication, Marriage)*

Dates used:_____

## Competition

The five-year-old ringbearer was obviously worried as he looked down the long aisle of the church where his aunt was to be married the following day. His grandmother had an idea. "I think I'll give a prize to the person who does the best job tomorrow," she told him.

The ringbearer's chin went up. There were fourteen others in the wedding party, not counting the minister. "I still think I can do it," he whispered.

The next day, the church filled, and the organ sounded triumphantly. When it was time, the little boy walked to the front with his head held high.

At the reception, when his grandmother told him he had won the prize, he was both excited and relieved.

"I was pretty sure I had it," he admitted, "until Aunt Dana came in wearing that white dress and the horn was blowing. Then I started thinking— she might win!"

—Barbara Lee
*(Marriage, Pride)*

Dates used:_____

"I take it there's something you haven't told me."

—Rob Portlock
*(Guilt, Privacy)*

Dates used:_____

## Courtesy

When my father was in the hospital, he had a stream of visitors from the church. One day two men stopped by. Their quiet conversation was interrupted by the other patient's peppery language from behind the curtain. Before leaving, the visitors read some Scripture and prayed.

After they left, the roommate loosed another string of expletives and then sheepishly confessed to Dad, "If I'd known one of those guys was a minister, I'd have watched my language."

"Oh," Dad replied, "they're the deacons in the church. I'm the minister."

—Ginny Dow
*(Guilt, Profanity)*

Dates used:_____

## Creation

Seen on a church sign: IF EVOLUTION IS TRUE, HOW COME MOTHERS STILL HAVE ONLY TWO HANDS?

—Donna Waldeyer
*(Evolution, Motherhood)*

Dates used:_____

# Crisis

A high-speed train was halted for several hours en route from Paris to Toulouse, France, when the emergency-stop mechanism jammed. An unidentified man had yanked it to stop the train because his wallet had fallen into a toilet, and when he reached to get it, his hand got stuck.

—Chuck Shepherd in *Pitch Weekly*
*(Emergencies, Teamwork)*

Dates used:_____

# Criticism

Winston Churchill was attending an official ceremony in London. Two men behind him recognized him and began to whisper behind his back.

"They say Churchill's quite senile now," said the one.

"Yes, they say he's doing England more harm than good," replied the other.

"They say he should step aside and leave the running of this government to younger, more dynamic people," continued the first man.

Churchill turned and in a loud voice said, "They also say he's quite deaf."

—Andrew Carr
*(Backbiting, Gossip)*

Dates used:_____

Every morning on our way to school, my kids and I pray. When I asked our 3-year-old if he wanted to pray, he promptly said, "God, please help Sissy not to suck her thumb."

To which Sissy quickly added, "And, God, please help my brother to stop reminding me."

—Linda Pace
*(Judging, Sin)*

Dates used:_____

## Crucifixion

The accounting department of a large insurance company was working on year-end reports when the computers went down. An emergency call was put in to the systems analyst. Busy with other troubleshooting, the man didn't appear until three hours later. Yet even then several clerks cheered, "He's here! Our savior!"

Without a word, the systems analyst turned to leave. Panicked, the accounting manager cried in alarm, "Where are you going?"

"I'm leaving," the analyst said with a smile. "I remember what they did to the last savior."

—Marla J. Kiley
*(Christ's Suffering, Easter)*

Dates used:_____

# Death

My five-year-old daughter and I often walked through an old cemetery to reach the local playground. One day she saw someone push a rod into the soil near a gravestone and hang a wreath on it.

"Why did that man put a wreath on the grave?" she asked.

"He wanted to remember the person who died," I replied.

"Will someone do that for me when I die?"

"I'm sure they will," I said, mentally preparing myself for the next question.

We walked in silence for a moment. Then she turned to me and said, "It won't be fair. All I'll see is the stick."

—Phoebe A. Johnson
*(Fairness, Perspective)*

Dates used:_____

Our son was five when his goldfish died. I agreed he could "send the goldfish back to God" any way he wanted. Expecting him to give the goldfish a proper burial in our flower garden, I was surprised to receive a call from our small, rural post office.

"Could you come over?" asked the postmaster. "I want to show you what Ben put in the mail drop." I walked quickly to the post office. She was waiting.

"Glenda, a lot is expected of the post office, but this is the most amazing delivery we have ever been asked to make!" She handed me the envelope, laughing.

On the outside of the envelope, printed in big, blue, capital letters were these words: TO GOD FROM BEN.

Inside the envelope was a very flat, dead goldfish.

—Glenda Barbre
*(Eternity, Mortality)*

Dates used:_____

## Decision-making

A telemarketer phones a home and says, "I'd like to talk to the person who makes the final purchasing decisions for your family."

The woman replies, "I'm sorry. That person is still at kindergarten and won't be home for another hour."

—*The Hope Health Letter*
*(Children, Influence)*

Dates used:_____

## Delegation

There are three ways to get something done:
1. Do it yourself.
2. Hire someone else to do it.
3. Forbid your kids to do it.

—*Homiletics*
*(Parenting, Workplace)*

Dates used:_____

# Devotions

During the day I take a few moments to unwind by reading the Bible. After seeing me do this for several years, my four-year-old daughter became concerned: "Aren't you ever going to get finished reading that book?"

—Jana Jones
*(Bible, Discipleship)*

Dates used:_____

# Disappointment

An Army Airborne ranger was learning to parachute. The sergeant barked out the orders:

1. Jump when you are told to jump.

2. Count to ten, then pull the ripcord.

3. If the first chute doesn't open, pull the second ripcord.

4. When you land, a truck will take you back to the post.

When the plane got over the landing zone, the soldier jumped when it was his turn. He counted to ten, then pulled the ripcord. Nothing happened. He pulled the second ripcord. Nothing happened.

"Oh great," he complained to himself. I'll bet the truck won't be waiting for us, either."

*(Complaining, Plans)*

Dates used:_____

# Discipleship

My friend decided it was time to talk to her bright four-year-old son, Benji, about receiving Christ.

"Benji," she asked quietly, "would you like to have Jesus in your heart?"

Benji rolled his blue eyes and answered seriously, "No. I don't think I want the responsibility."

—Brenda Goodine
*(Evangelism, Responsibility)*

Dates used:_____

"Forget your wife's warnings—tell the joke."

—Dik LaPine
*(Influence, Sin)*

Dates used:_____

56

# Doubt

The only thing that casts doubt on the miracles of Jesus is that they were all witnessed by fishermen.

—A Wisconsin fishing guide
*(Inerrancy, Miracles)*

Dates used:_____

# Easter

My Sunday school class of kindergarteners was studying the Creation story. After several weeks, we were ready to review.

"What did God make the first day?" I quizzed. "The second day?" They answered both questions correctly.

"And what happened on the third day?" I asked.

One little child, face shining with enthusiasm, exclaimed, "He rose from the dead!"

—Michele L. Hardie
*(Creation, Resurrection)*

Dates used:_____

# Employers

Scott Adams, creator of the *Dilbert* cartoon strip, conducted his Second Annual "Highly Unscientific Dilbert Survey," asking this question:

"If you had a chance to hit your boss in the back of the head with one of the following objects, with no risk of getting caught, which would you use?" Here are the percentages for respondents' answers:

A large bean burrito—19 percent

"Nerf" ball—17

Ripe melon—14

Framed certificate of appreciation—13

Outdated computer you are forced to use—13

Your last performance review, including the 600-pound filing cabinet you keep it in—13

All your co-workers, bound by duct tape and flung from a huge catapult—8

A Ford Pinto with a full tank of gas—7

"I think the bean burrito won because it would make a really cool sound and it would be messy with or without guacamole," said Adams. Over 64 percent of respondents selected a non-lethal response, knowing if their boss were injured, it would mean more work for them.

—Lynn Walford for UPI

*(Frustration, Work)*

Dates used:_____

60

A large corporation recently installed a stray dog as a senior vice-president. The announcement in the company bulletin read, "His ability to get along with anyone, his prompt response to a pat on the back, his interest in watching others work, and his great knack for looking wise while saying nothing make him a natural for this position."

*—Quote Digest*
*(Cooperation, Wisdom)*

Dates used:_____

# Evangelism

Officer Tori Matthews of the Southern California Humane Society got an emergency call: a boy's pet iguana had been scared up a tree by a neighbor's dog. It then fell from the tree into a swimming pool, where it sank like a brick. Officer Matthews came with her net. She dived into the pool, emerging seconds later with the pet's limp body.

As the *Arizona Republic* (2/14/95) reported, she thought, *Well, you do* CPR *on a person and a dog, why not an iguana?* So she locked lips with the lizard.

"Now that I look back on it," she said, "it was a pretty ugly animal to be kissing, but the last thing I wanted to do was tell this little boy that his iguana had died." The lizard responded to her efforts and is expected to make a full recovery.

Tori Matthews didn't see a water-logged reptile; she saw a little boy's beloved pet. We may never see the beauty in some people, but when we realize how much they mean to God, we'll do what we can to keep them from drowning.

*(Compassion, Missions)*

Dates used:_____

FORMER AMWAY REPRESENTATIVE CLAUDE HOFFENPOPPER TEACHES EVANGELISM

"You don't have to lead anyone to Christ personally; you just need to sign up ten people who will, who'll sign up ten more people, who'll ..."

—Steve Phelps
*(Recruiting, Witnessing)*

Dates used:_____

After listening to Chuck Swindoll on the radio, eight-year-old Debbie asked six-year-old David, "Do you know about Jesus?"

Expecting a new slant on the old story, David replied, "No."

Sister continued, "Sit still because this is really scary." After explaining the gospel as only an 8-year-old could, she popped the question.

"Now David, when you die, do you want to go to heaven to be with Jesus, God, your Mommy and Daddy and big sister, or do you want to go to the lake of fire to be with the Devil and bank robbers?"

David thought a moment, then replied, "I want to stay right here."

—Jim Abrahamson
*(Contentment, Worldliness)*

Dates used:_____

A man who was trying to be more diligent about witnessing saw an opportunity when he was standing in the "10 Items or Less" checkout at the grocery store.

"All have sinned," he began, sincerely looking at the clerk scanning his items.

"Including you, Mac," she replied, without looking up. "I count twelve items here."

—Mary Chambers
*(Honesty, Integrity)*

Dates used:_____

The songleader asked the congregation to turn in their hymnals and sing, "Till the Whole World Knows." My daughter whispered, "I think we're going to be here a *long* time."

—Melodie Dean
*(Missions, Music)*

Dates used:_____

A woman bought a parrot to keep her company. She took him home, but returned the bird to the store the next day. "This bird doesn't talk," she told the owner.

"Does he have a mirror in his cage?" asked the owner. "Parrots love mirrors. They see themselves in the mirror and start up a conversation." The woman bought a mirror and left. The next day, she returned. The bird still wasn't talking.

"How about a ladder? Parrots love walking up and down a ladder. A happy parrot is more likely to talk." The woman bought a ladder and left. Sure enough, she was back the next day; the bird still wasn't talking.

"Does your parrot have a swing? If not, that's the problem. He'll relax and talk up a storm." The woman reluctantly bought a swing and left.

When she walked into the store the next day, her countenance had changed. "The parrot died," she said. The pet store owner was shocked.

"I'm so sorry. Tell me, did he ever say a word?" he asked.

"Yes, right before he died," the woman replied. "He said, 'Don't they sell any food at that pet store?' "

*(Materialism, Priorities)*

Dates used:_____

# Example

Our Sunday school teacher was a quiet, godly man with a quick wit. Reflecting on one of the verses in our lesson, "Abstain from all appearance of evil," he said with a chuckle, "But please don't do as I do—do what I say." He then explained with a smile, "I was on my way into the post office when I spotted a beer can on the sidewalk. I picked it up to throw it away. Turning around too fast, I momentarily lost my balance and with the empty beer can clutched in my hand proceeded to stumble and trip the whole way up the front steps."

—Betty Traver
*(Appearances, Role Models)*

Dates used:_____

# Faith

We were driving through Pennsylvania Dutch Country with my daughter and her seven-year-old son. We passed an Amish horse and buggy, and my grandson's curiosity was stirred.

"Why do they use horses instead of automobiles?"

My daughter explained that the Amish didn't believe in automobiles.

After a few moments, he asked: "But can't they see them?"

—Harold F. Bermel
*(Belief, Trust)*

Dates used:_____

"I've stopped expecting you to make leaps of faith, but it would be nice to see a hop now and then."

—Doug Hall
*(Doubt, Pessimism)*

Dates used:_____

## Fatherhood

Our granddaughter's second-grade class was asked to write about their personal heroes. Her father was flattered to find out that she had chosen him. "Why did you pick me?" he asked her later.

"Because I couldn't spell Arnold Schwarzenegger," she replied.

—Jack Eppolito
*(Heroes, Honesty)*

Dates used:_____

## Forgiveness

One Saturday morning I awoke to the delightful smell of waffles and the sound of our two small boys in the kitchen with my husband. Padding down to breakfast, I sat on my husband's lap and gave him a big hug for his thoughtfulness.

Later that day, we were having a heated discussion in our bedroom when our four-year-old, Jacob, stopped us in midsentence. Standing in the doorway, he said, "Mommy, try to remember how you felt when you were on Daddy's lap."

—Jane Schmidt
*(Example, Love)*

Dates used:_____

During Sunday school, I was trying to teach the children that we all need God's forgiveness. After the Bible story, I asked one of the girls, "Lisa, when is a time you might need God's forgiveness?"

Her blank stare prompted a response from my son. "It's okay, Lisa. You don't have to tell her."

Then he turned to me and said, "We don't have to tell you our problems. This isn't the Oprah Winfrey Show."

—Ranai Carlton
*(Confession, Repentance)*

Dates used:_____

## Free Will

When my daughter was five, she disobeyed me and had been sent to her room. After a few minutes, I went in to have a talk about why she was being punished. Teary-eyed, she asked, "Why do we do wrong things?"

"Well," I said, "Sometimes the Devil tells us to do something wrong and we listen to him. We need to learn to listen to God instead."

To which she sobbed, "But God doesn't talk loud enough!"

—Jo M. Guerrero
*(God's Direction, Prayer)*

Dates used:_____

## Frugality

Save a little money each and every month, and at the end of the year, you'll be surprised at just how little you have.

—Ernest Haskins in *Quote*
*(Money, Savings)*

Dates used:_____

## Fruit of the Spirit

Our young daughter was learning the fruit of the Spirit, so I asked her to recite them to me. "Love, joy, peace, patience, kindness, goodness, faithfulness, gentleness, and *remote* control!" was her reply.

—Laura Smith
*(Self-Control, Television)*

Dates used:_____

# Giving

For years we lived in a small town with one bank and three churches. Early one Monday morning, the bank called all three churches with the same request: "Could you bring in Sunday's collection right away? We're out of $1 bills."

—Clara Null
*(Miserliness, Stewardship)*

Dates used:_____

# God's Call

Having lived in South America as missionaries, my family and I realized that moving to another jungle location meant a lot of work. We knew the discomforts of such things as snakes and bugs.

One morning, a few days after beginning to clean our temporary home, the family and I were taking a short break. While we were drinking tea, a large black beetle suddenly flew through the room with a loud buzzing noise. As it darted between us, my wife let out a startled scream.

Astonished more by her scream than the beetle, my youngest daughter cried out, "For heaven's sake, Mom!"

My wife resolutely replied, "That's the only reason I'm here."

—Patrick Jenkins
*(Heaven, Missions)*

Dates used:_____

## God's Image

My husband admired our six-year-old daughter while she was dancing around the kitchen. Finally, he stopped her with a hug.

"You know," he said, looking Amy in the eyes, "you're cute—just like your father."

Amy was silent for a moment. "You mean my heavenly Father or you?"     —Jane Stanford
*(Beauty, Fathers)*

Dates used:_____

## God's Love

My Sunday school class of youngsters had some problems repeating the Lord's Prayer. One child prayed, "Our Father, who art in heaven, how'd you know my name."

—Clara Null
*(Children, Prayer)*

Dates used:_____

76

In the 1980s, people shelled out thousands of dollars to own a pot-bellied pig, an exotic house pet imported from Vietnam. Their breeders claimed these mini-pigs were quite smart and would grow to only forty pounds. Well, they were half right. The pigs were smart. But they had a tendency to grow to about 150 pounds and become quite aggressive.

What do people do with an unwanted pot-bellied pig? Fortunately, Dale Riffle came to the rescue. Someone had given Riffle one of these pigs, and he fell in love with it. The pig, Rufus, never learned to use its litter box and developed this craving for carpets and wallpaper and drywall. Yet Riffle sold his suburban home and moved with Rufus to a five-acre farm in West Virginia. He started taking in other unwanted pigs, and before long, the guy was living in hog heaven.

There are currently 180 residents on his farm. According to an article in *U.S. News & World Report,* they snooze on beds of pine shavings. They wallow in mud puddles. They soak in plastic swimming pools and listen to piped-in classical music. And they never need fear that one day they'll become bacon or pork chops. There's actually a waiting list of unwanted pigs trying to get a hoof in the door at Riffle's farm. *(continued)*

Dale Riffle told the reporter, "We're all put on earth for some reason, and I guess pigs are my lot in life." How could anybody in his right mind fall in love with pigs?

I'll tell you something even more amazing. An infinite, perfectly holy, majestic, awesome God is passionately in love with insignificant, sinful, sometimes openly rebellious, frequently indifferent people. God loves people like you and me.

—Jim Nicodem on *Preaching Today*
*(Fatherhood, Grace)*

Dates used:_____

## God's Omniscience

A large bowl of Red Delicious apples was placed at the front of the cafeteria line at Asbury College. The note attached read, "Take only one please, God is watching."

Some prankster attached a note to a tray of peanut butter cookies at the other end of the line that said, "Take all you want. God is watching the apples."

—Tom Allen
*(College, Greed)*

Dates used:_____

## God's Wrath

I was listening to my five-year-old son, Matthew, as he worked on his Speak-and-Spell computer. He was concentrating intensely, typing words for the computer to say back to him.

Matthew punched in the word *God.* To his surprise, the computer said, "Word not found."

He tried again with the same reply. With great disgust, he stared at the computer and told it in no uncertain terms, "Jesus is not going to like this!"

—Mary Farwell
*(Culture, Godlessness)*

Dates used:_____

When I was a young, single mom with four children, it was difficult to get them all ready for church on Sunday. One particular Sunday morning as the children started to complain and squabble, I stomped from one room to the other, saying out loud why it was important we go to church as a family and have a good attitude. Suddenly, I noticed all four children huddled together and laughing. "What's so funny?" I asked.

"Mom," they said, "every time you slam down your foot, smoke comes out. It must be the wrath of God!" In reality, it was the powder I had sprinkled in my shoes.

But it worked. We made it to church that morning and practically every Sunday thereafter.

—Mary Jane Kurtz
*(Parenting, Persuasion)*

Dates used:_____

## Grace

Heaven goes by favor. If it went by merit, you would stay out, and your dog would go in.

—Mark Twain
*(Favor, Works)*

Dates used:_____

## Greed

At a birthday party, it came time to serve the cake. A little boy named Brian blurted out, "I want the biggest piece!"

His mother quickly scolded him. "Brian, it's not polite to ask for the biggest piece."

The little guy looked at her in confusion, and asked, "Well then, how *do* you get it?"

—Olive Freeman
*(Covetousness, Selfishness)*

Dates used:_____

"Besides calling every Sunday 'Easter,' does anyone else have ideas for improving church attendence?."

—Tim Liston
*(Committees, Easter)*

Dates used:_____

# Guilt

After a man died, the attorney said to his wife, "He did not leave a will. So we need to know the last words he ever said to you."

She said, "I don't want to tell you."

He said, "Look, he did not leave a will. We need to know the last words he ever said to you."

She said, "I don't want to tell you. It was something between the two of us."

He said, "May I beg you one more time?"

She said, "Well, if you have to know, I'll tell you. The last thing he ever said to me was, 'You don't scare me. You couldn't hit the broad side of a barn with that old gun.' "

—Larry Moyer
*(Incrimination, Indictment)*

Dates used:_____

# Hardheartedness

These days, not everyone has compassion. Recently I heard about the Psychiatric Hotline. When I dialed the number, I received the following menu of options:

If you are obsessive-compulsive, please press 1 repeatedly.

If you are codependent, please ask someone to press 2.

If you have multiple personalities, please press 3, 4, 5, and 6.

If you are schizophrenic, listen carefully and a little voice will tell you which number to press.

If you are paranoid-delusional, we know who you are and what you want. Just stay on the line while we trace this call.

—James Brown
*(Compassion, Helpfulness)*

Dates used:_____

## Health

Cheerful people resist disease better than glum ones. In other words, the surly bird catches the germ.

—*The Hope Health Letter* (4/96)
*(Attitude, Optimism)*

Dates used:_____

## Heaven

One Sunday morning the pastor read John 14:2 to the congregation using a modern translation. His version read, "In my Father's house there are many dwelling places."

Immediately an elderly lady stood up and said, "I want you to read that Scripture again—from my Bible. I've lived in old, run-down houses all my life, and I'm looking forward to that mansion!"

—Carol Reddekop
*(Bible, Expectations)*

Dates used:_____

My brother and his new wife were escorted to their bridal suite in an elegant hotel in the wee hours of the morning. They were tired from the many hours at their wedding reception and from mingling with their guests. They took a look around their room, taking in the sofa, chairs, and table. But where was the bed? This was the bridal suite?

Then they discovered the sofa was a hide-a-bed, complete with lumpy mattress and springs sagging to the floor. My brother and his new wife spent a fitful night on the hide-a-bed, waking up with sore backs.

The next morning, the new husband went to the hotel desk and gave the management a tongue-lashing for giving them such a terrible room for the bridal suite.

"Did you open the door in the room?" was the response.

When my brother went back up to the room, he opened a door they had thought was the closet. There, complete with fruit baskets and chocolates, was a beautiful bedroom.

—Cynthia Thomas
*(Abundant Life, Expectations)*

Dates used:_____

# Home

During World War II when housing was in short supply, a lady in our church told a five-year-old girl, "It's too bad you folks don't have a home."

The child quickly replied, "We have a home. We just don't have a house to put it in!"

—Margaret T. Hiscox
*(Family, Love)*

Dates used:_____

# Honesty

A woman leaving the worship service said to the minister, "I enjoyed the sermon."

"Don't thank me. Thank the Lord," said the minister.

"It wasn't *that* good," the lady replied.

—Robert S. Smith
*(Compliments, Humility)*

Dates used:_____

Two brothers had terrorized a small town for decades. They were unfaithful to their wives, abusive to their children, and dishonest in business. Then the younger brother died unexpectedly.

The surviving brother went to the pastor of the local church. "I want you to conduct my brother's funeral," he said, "but it's important to me that during the service, you tell everyone my brother was a saint."

"But he was far from that," the minister countered.

The wealthy brother pulled out his checkbook. "Reverend, I'm prepared to give $100,000 to your church. All I'm asking is that you publicly state that my brother was a saint."

On the day of the funeral, the pastor began his eulogy this way. "Everyone here knows that the deceased was a wicked man, a womanizer, and a drunk. He terrorized his employees and cheated on his taxes." Then he paused.

"But as evil and sinful as this man was, compared to his older brother, he was a saint!"

—Greg Asimakoupoulos
*(Comparison, Temptation)*

Dates used:_____

The *Sweet's Soul Cafe* newsletter included this list of "Top 10 Liars' Lies":

10. We'll stay only five minutes.
9. This will be a short meeting.
8. I'll respect you in the morning.
7. The check is in the mail.
6. I'm from the government, and I'm here to help you.
5. This hurts me more than it hurts you.
4. Your money will be cheerfully refunded.
3. We service what we sell.
2. Your table will be ready in just a minute.
1. I'll start exercising (dieting, forgiving) tomorrow.

—Leonard Sweet
*(Dishonesty, Lying)*

Dates used:_____

# Humility

In seminary I was impressed with the way Jesus used unusual means to make powerful points—for instance, riding into Jerusalem on a donkey.

I tried taking my cue from Jesus in my first church after seminary. I figured communication would be enhanced by working with live animals.

Like a turtle. A turtle makes progress only if it dares stick out its neck. That's a pretty good posture for Jesus' disciples, too, I thought.

So, my first week there, I asked the kids to find me a turtle. That week, some girls found a turtle and brought it to church, and an elderly couple, while taking a drive in the country, had to slam on the brakes as a turtle ambled across the road.

Eureka! I had two turtles!

The next Sunday I stood before the congregation, trying to exude proper Princeton decorum. In my black Geneva gown accented by red piping, I called the small fries forward and began my talk.

As I held up one turtle, I tapped on its shell. He ducked into it, obviously not going anywhere. "That's like a person acting as if Jesus weren't walking beside him," I observed.

*(continued)*

The turtle, meanwhile, got a bad case of nerves and in front of the whole congregation, urinated all over my new robe.

The congregation howled. I acted as though I were not drenched and quickly returned the turtle to his box, commenting that strange faces do funny things to shy turtles.

Picking up the second turtle, I started again. I tapped on the shell, this time holding it well away from my robe. The turtle ducked inside and . . . held its composure. Relieved, I asked, "What happens to a turtle that refuses to stick out its neck?"

A tyke shot up his hand, exclaiming, "It goes tinkle-tinkle!"

That brought the house down again. I thought my ministry had been destroyed in its second week. But the nervous turtle made people see that their new preacher was all too human. And they accepted me, stains and all— though they did tend to shy away from my new robe.

—Jack R. Van Ens

*(Embarrassment, Pride)*

Dates used:_____

I once pastored a church that met in a former dance hall. Wanting to save money, our small fellowship used carpet remnants for the center aisle. Over the years, the seams began to loosen, and if you weren't careful, your foot could catch.

My wife told me, "Honey, you should get those fixed before some elderly lady trips and falls." I applied a procedure I had learned from my deacons. I tabled the issue.

A few weeks later before a Sunday morning service, I was meditating in my office at the rear of the church. Realizing I was a few minutes late, I hurried into the sanctuary and briskly walked up the center aisle.

As I reached the front, in full view of the congregation, my foot slipped under a loose seam, and I lunged forward. Fortunately, I caught my balance, but my toupee decided to embark on a journey of its own. I snatched it in midair, deposited it back on my head, and proceeded calmly and coolly to the pulpit.

When I turned around, however, I was greeted with mass hysteria. I had placed my toupee on sideways!

Besides the important lesson of listening to the cautions of your wife, I learned something else: If it's not your own hair, don't wear it.

—Jerry Lambert
*(Embarrassment, Honesty)*

Dates used:_____

A sign on a department store dressing room mirror:

"Objects in mirror may appear bigger than they actually are."

—*The Hope Health Letter* (12/95)
*(Distortion, Spiritual Blindness)*

Dates used:_____

## Impatience

A young woman's car stalled at a stoplight. She tried to get it started, but nothing would happen. The light turned green, and there she sat, angry and embarrassed, holding up traffic. The car behind could have gone around, but instead the driver added to her anger by laying on his horn.

After another desperate attempt to get the car started, she got out and walked back to the honker. The man rolled down his window in surprise.

"Tell you what," she said. "You go start my car, and I'll sit back here and honk the horn for you."

*(Criticism, Patience)*

Dates used:_____

## Inadequacy

Two cows were grazing in a pasture when they saw a milk truck pass. On the side of the truck were the words, "Pasteurized, homogenized, standardized, Vitamin A added."

One cow sighed and said to the other, "Makes you feel kind of inadequate, doesn't it?"
—John Maxwell, *The Winning Attitude*
*(Contentment, Inferiority)*

Dates used:_____

## Incarnation

One evening my three-year-old son and I were sitting at the dinner table looking outside at the birds. I began telling him interesting facts about our feathered friends.

Suddenly, my son looked me square in the eye and said, "How do you know? Were you a bird once?"
—Deb Kallman
*(Evangelism, Missions)*

Dates used:_____

"Pastor, we've put up with praise choruses,
worship bands, interpretive dance,
and you preaching in blue jeans,
but we draw the line at bungee baptisms."

—Steve Phelps
*(Baptism, Boards)*

Dates used:_____

## Insensitivity

A cartoon showed a man leaning over a cas-
ket, whispering last words to the deceased:
"Does this mean you won't be cooking dinner
tonight?"

—Tim Ayers

*(Dependence, Marriage)*

Dates used:_____

# Jobs

Buffalo Bills offensive lineman Glenn Parker speculated as to why NFL linemen are generally cheerful: "There are not a lot of well-paying jobs for 300-pounders. We found one, and we're happy about it."

—*Chicago Tribune*
*(Contentment, Happiness)*

Dates used:_____


The human resources director was taken back by the applicant's salary request. "You certainly expect to be compensated well for a beginner."

The applicant replied, "Well sure. Work's a lot harder when you don't know what you're doing."

*(Expectations, Work)*

Dates used:_____

A job applicant was asked, "Why were you discharged from your last position?"

The reply, "I was overly ambitious. I wanted to take work home with me."

The next question, "Who was your employer?"

"First National Bank."

*(Integrity, Stealing)*

Dates used:_____

## Judging Others

Not long ago I had a kidney stone but was able to pass it. A few months later, my husband also passed a kidney stone. I made sure to remind him, "The Bible says, 'Let she who is without sin cast the first stone.' "

—Judie Larson
*(Compassion, Sin)*

Dates used:_____

The first assignment for my husband, Cecil, in his art class was to sketch the San Luis Rey mission in Oceanside, California.

Everyone turned in a sketch, and the teacher began his oral critique of each student's work. When he came to Cecil's, he held it up and said, "Who is the figure in the doorway of the mission?"

"That's the padre, sir."

"Well, don't you think your padre looks a little sick?"

"He could be," Cecil responded. "I'm an artist, not a doctor."

—Agnes Goddard
*(Criticism, Perspective)*

Dates used:_____

# Knowing God

One day my four-year-old son asked me about God's name. I explained God had many names, including Father, Lord, and Jehovah.

After listening to my long explanation, my son asked, "Can I just call him Steve?"

—Vicki Crooks
*(God, Intimacy)*

Dates used:_____

# Leadership

Our church has several pastors, each with a specific title such as Senior Pastor, Pastor of Caring and Fellowship, and so on. When my wife worked in the church office, a woman came in to see the Pastor of Missions. Searching her mind for the exact title, she became momentarily confused and asked the church receptionist, "May I see the Minister of Passion?"

—Bo Kaufmann
*(Missions, Staff Relations)*

Dates used:_____

# Dieting Religiously

I try to live by the book and when it came to losing those pesky pounds this spring I decided to diet by the book, taking cues from scripture.

I buffeted my body daily (accompanied by praise tapes).

Locust & wild honey were out of the question, but I did shun fat ("All fat belongs to the Lord" Lev. 3:16) and chewed each bite forty times (the number of testing & tribulation).

106

# Love

A husband asked his wife, "Tell me, Dear, have you ever been in love before?"

She thought a moment and replied, "No, Darling. I once respected a man for his great intelligence. I admired another for his remarkable courage. I was captivated by yet another for his good looks and charm. But with you, well, how else could you explain it, except love?"

*(Admiration, Marriage)*

Dates used:_____

From the Internet, some advice from kids on love and romance:

*How do people in love typically behave?*

"Mooshy . . . like puppy dogs . . . except puppy dogs don't wag their tails so much" (Arnold, age 10).

"When a person gets kissed for the first time, they fall down and don't get up for at least an hour" (Wendy, age 8).

*Why do people in love hold hands?*

"They want to make sure their rings don't fall off because they paid good money for them" (Gavin, age 8).

"They are just practicing for when they might have to walk down the aisle someday and do the holy matchimony thing" (John, age 9).

*(continued)*

*Confidential opinions about love.*

"Love is foolish . . . but I still might try it sometime" (Jill, age 6).

"Love will find you even if you're trying to hide from it. I been trying to hide from it since I was five, but the girls keep finding me" (Dave, age 8).

"I'm not rushing into love. Fourth grade is hard enough" (Regina, age 10).

*What are some ways to make someone fall in love with you?*

"Tell them that you own a whole bunch of candy stores" (Del, age 6).

"Don't do things like have smelly, green sneakers. You might get attention, but attention ain't the same thing as love" (Alonzo, age 9).

*Tell us your thoughts on kissing.*

"You learn it right on the spot when the gooshy feelings get the best of you" (Brian, age 7).

"If it's your mom, you can kiss her anytime. But if it's a new person, you better ask for permission" (Roger, age 6).

"I look at it like this: Kissing is fine if you like it, but it's a free country and nobody should be forced to do it" (Billy, age 6).

*(Romance, Valentine's Day)*

Dates used:_____

## Marriage

While browsing in a Christian bookstore one day, I discovered a shelf of reduced-price items. Among the gifts was a little figurine of a man and woman, their heads lovingly tilted toward one another. HAPPY 10TH ANNIVERSARY read the inscription. It appeared to be in perfect condition, yet its tag indicated DAMAGED.

Examining it more closely, I found another tag underneath that read: WIFE IS COMING UNGLUED.

—Gayle Urban
*(Commitment, Stress)*

Dates used:_____

A young bride complained to her friend, "My husband and I are getting along together fairly well, but he simply can't bear children."

"Oh well," a friend consoled her. "You can't expect men to do everything."

*(Children, Parenting)*

Dates used:_____

I was issuing a marriage license one day when the bride-to-be exploded.

"You rat! You told me this was your first marriage!"

"It is!"

"Oh yeah? Where it says, 'number of marriages,' you wrote 'two'!"

"Oh ... I thought that meant how many people were getting married."

—Ida M. Pardue
*(Divorce, Weddings)*

Dates used:_____

The caption of an A. A. McCourt cartoon, in the *National Review*, had the wife speaking to the husband, "There you go again, quoting our marriage vows out of context!"

*(Arguing, Disharmony)*

Dates used:_____

# Men and Women

One little girl sang a slightly different version of the Gloria Patri one Sunday morning:

"World with weird men, Amen! Amen!"

—Deanna Hendersen
*(Music, Worship)*

Dates used:_____

In 1492, Columbus set out for the Orient and ended up in the Caribbean, thus setting a pattern that has continued for over 500 years. Men still won't stop and ask for directions.

*(Pride, Self-reliance)*

Dates used:_____

"So far, the only thing we have in common is
an aversion to signing, socalizing, and sharing."

—Erik Johnson
*(Church, Fellowship)*

Dates used:_____

# Ministry

A woman answered the knock at her door to find an obviously destitute man who wanted to earn some money by doing odd jobs. She was touched by his need and asked, "Can you paint?"

"Yes," he said. "I'm a pretty good painter."

"Well, here's a gallon of green paint and a brush. Go around the house and you'll see a porch that needs repainting. Be very careful. When you're done, I'll look it over and pay you what it's worth."

It wasn't more than an hour before he knocked again. "All finished," he reported.

"Did you do a good job?" she asked.

"Yes. But Lady, there's one thing I'd like to point out to you. That's not a Porsche back there. That's a Mercedes."

We don't always get what we expect when we invest in the lives of others.

—Bruce Thielemann
*(Communication, Expectations)*

Dates used:_____

## Missions

At 18, I went to a remote mission outpost in Africa for a short-term project. Upon our arrival, I was instructed my sleeping quarters were in the church, so I placed my cot in front of the pulpit and turned in for the night.

Within minutes, several folks had slipped into the church. I lay motionless on my portable bed, staring straight up. Could it be? Yes, there was a service that night. The church was packed!

Finally, the pastor arrived, went behind the pulpit and started the service, graciously ignoring me. Then a youth ensemble came forward, formed a half-circle just in front of me, and sang.

Soon the service ended. I realized there was nothing I could do, so I sat up in my pajamas and shook hands with the people as they left.

—Doug A. Schneider
*(Cross-Cultural Ministry, Manners)*

Dates used:_____

"You're touching the world with your ministry, Pastor.
Your luggage is in Malaysia, your Bible is in China,
and your sermon is in Omaha."

—Jonny Hawkins
*(Ministry, Travel)*

Dates used:_____

Many years ago when my brothers were small, one of them said to the other, "I'm going to eat you!"

My mother overheard and said, "Oh, we don't eat people. There are some people who eat other people. We call them cannibals. Someone should tell them about Jesus."

To which David replied, "Well, they'd better tell them over the telephone."

—Miriam Martin
*(Evangelism, Fear)*

Dates used:_____

## Mortality

To begin a discussion on values, our youth pastor asked the teens this question: "What would you do if your doctor told you you had only twenty-four hours to live?"

The teens' responses were typically, "Be with friends and family." But the discussion came undone when Jason, our thirteen-year-old, said, "I'd get a second opinion."

—Donna Spratt
*(Calm, Death)*

Dates used:_____

# Motherhood

My mother was baby-sitting my son, Dirk, at her house one day. When I stopped to pick him up, Mom told me that Dirk had followed her into the bedroom as she put some things away in the closet. "Grandma," he asked, "what room is this?"

"This is a closet, Dirk," she explained.

"We don't have a room like this in our house," he said.

"Of course you do," she insisted. "You have lots of closets at your home."

When he again denied having closets at our house, she tried another tack. "Where do you keep all your clothes?" she asked.

He replied, "In the dryer."

—Shari Hanson
*(Busyness, Tidiness)*

Dates used:_____

Lisa covers all her bases before she sings her solo

"Pastor just asked me to sing this morning ...
I have a terrible sore throat ...
My dog died this morning before–*sniff*–church ..."

—Steve Phelps
*(Excuses, Singing)*

Dates used:_____

# Neighbors

Upon arriving in our new home in Kentucky, my seven-year-old son, Jason, decided to explore the neighborhood. He was back within the hour proclaiming that he had made some new friends.

"Good. Are they boys or girls?" I asked.

"One is a boy, and one is a girl," he replied.

"That's great," I said. "How old are they?"

"Mom," my son replied, "that would be very rude to ask."

I was puzzled by his response, but about an hour later, Jason was back. "Mom!" he shouted through the screen door. "I found out how old my new friends are. The girl is 65, and the boy is 70."

—Teri Leinbaugh
*(Aging, Friendship)*

Dates used:_____

## New Year's Day

Here are some bold prophecies for the year ahead:

Chuck Swindoll will author a best-selling book.

Significant church-state issues will be debated in the nation's courts.

The head of a major parachurch group will name a family member to succeed him.

A leading television evangelist will appeal for money.

A new, "finally understandable" version of the Bible will be published.

A presidential candidate will try to curry favor among Christians.

Don't ask me how I do it.

—Eutychus in *Christianity Today*
*(Certainty, Prophecy)*

Dates used:_____

## Optimism

An optimist is someone who:

Sets up *all* the folding chairs for Wednesday night Bible study!

Makes plans to meet his spouse at 8:45 after an 8 o'clock board meeting!

Puts her shoes back on when the minister says, "In conclusion. . ."!

—Mary Chambers
*(Expectations, Hope)*

Dates used:_____

# Panic

In *Lead On,* John Haggai tells the story of Mrs. Monroe in Darlington, Maryland. The mother of eight children, she came home one afternoon from the grocery store and noticed it was a bit quieter than usual.

She looked in the living room and five of her darlings were sitting in a circle. She put down the groceries, walked over, and saw they were playing with five of the cutest skunks you can imagine.

She was instantly terrified, and she screamed, "Run children, run!" Each child grabbed a skunk and ran, in five different directions. Her screams so scared the children that each one squeezed his skunk!

It's always too soon to panic.

*(Afflictions, Trials)*

Dates used:_____

# Another Baby?

There's a difference between your first pregnancy and subsequent ones—beginning with how people respond. . .

You're less concerned about "losing your figure" (it's gone) and just look forward to not holding your stomach in. . .

You can wear most of your own clothes since you haven't worn a shirt that tucks in or a dress with a waist since before the last baby. . .

YABADABADOO!

Your husband is more relaxed during labor. . .

. . . and with your first you read every book about pregnancy and babies you could get your hands on—now you feel as if you could write one.

After I had related how tough I had it as a kid, my six-year-old son Jason put his arm around me and said, "It's all right, Dad. You're living with us now."

—Jack Eppolito
*(Hardships, Reminiscence)*

Dates used:_____


Did you know there's a special chain letter for parents? It reads:

Dear Friend: This chain letter is meant to bring relief and happiness to you. Unlike other chain letters, this one does not cost money. Simply send a copy of this letter to six other parents who are tired of their teenagers. Then bundle yours up and send him or her to the parent at the bottom of the list.

In one week, you will receive 16,436 teenagers—and one of them should be worth keeping. Warning: One dad broke the chain and got his own teenager back.

—Roger Poupart
*(Contentment, Teenagers)*

Dates used:_____

## Pastoral Care

A troubled parishioner sought counsel from his minister:

"Pastor, everyone calls me a liar."

"Oh, come on now," said the pastor. "I can't believe that."

—*The Light* (Issue 11)
*(Counseling, Lying)*

Dates used:_____

## Patience

One time a warden asked a man on death row what he would like to eat for his last meal.

The inmate said, "I would like to have a huge piece of watermelon."

The warden said, "You must be kidding? This is December. Watermelons have not been planted, let alone harvested."

The inmate said, "That's okay. I don't mind waiting."

—Larry Moyer
*(Delay, Procrastination)*

Dates used:_____

# Peacemaking

When I was a teenager, our family took cross-country car trips each summer. To keep the peace, we each took a turn choosing a cassette to play in the car tape deck. No one was allowed to complain or comment about another's choice.

My mother liked to listen to hymns. I chose contemporary Christian music. My younger brother preferred rock. And Dad? He always thought the best thing was a 90-minute tape that was still blank!

—Sharon Fleming
*(Respect, Silence)*

Dates used:_____

# Peer Pressure

The "Just say No" slogan seems to have caught on and helped the fight against drugs.

I've been so impressed by the concept that I've started a small group in our church based on the same principle: "Just say no when you really want to." The group has attracted a variety of people. The chairman of our Constitutional Revision Subcommittee, the former leader of our "Interpreting Revelation" study, and the chaperones from our "Junior High Goes Crazy" weekend retreat have all been regular attendees. And while no one admits being there to resist financial commitments, the subject of pledging does seem to come up quite often.

Two of our long-time board members and our pastor's wife considered joining for a while, but I think their sense of guilt or commitment was too strong. They started their own, "Just Say Maybe" group, and in almost no time, most of our group switched over.

But the "Just Say No" group will go on. After all, there's still me and the judge from last year's Pie Bake.

—Eutychus in *Christianity Today*
*(Committees, Small Groups)*

Dates used:_____

131

## Perseverance

A young woman from our congregation wrote me from graduate school. She reported on her studies and extra-curricular activities, which included participating in a Weight Watchers group.

Determined to lose weight, she had set a goal of losing 78 pounds. In fact, she wrote, she had already lost 16. But then she added the Bible reference John 6:9. I checked my Bible and read with a smile, "But what are they among so many?"

—Guy D. Mattox, Jr.
*(Dedication, Discipline)*

Dates used:_____

I had decided to retire from the ministry, and one Sunday I explained my decision to the congregation: "I wear two hearing aids and tri-focal glasses; I have a partial plate and I sometimes walk with a cane. It seems to me," I concluded, "that the Lord is telling me it's time to retire."

After the service, a white-haired lady told me, "Reverend, you have misinterpreted what the Lord has been saying to you. He's not telling you it's time to retire; he's telling you that if you keep going, he'll keep you patched up."

—Ivan P. Downing
*(Health, Ministry)*

Dates used:_____

## Popularity

In April 1993, just after Steve Morrow scored the goal that gave the Arsenal Team England's League Cup soccer championship, his teammates tossed him into the air in ritual celebration of their victory. However, they failed to catch him when he came down, and Morrow was carried off the field on a stretcher with a broken arm and an oxygen mask on his face.

—Chuck Shepherd in *Pitch Weekly*
*(Leadership, Recognition)*

Dates used:_____

133

# Prayer

When a nightclub opened on Main Street, the only church in that small town organized an all-night prayer meeting. The members asked God to burn down the club. Within a few minutes, lightning struck the club, and it burned to the ground. The owner sued the church, which denied responsibility.

After hearing both sides, the judge said, "It seems that wherever the guilt may lie, the nightclub owner believes in prayer, while the church doesn't."

—Herb Miller in *Connecting with God*
*(Faith, Responsibility)*

Dates used:_____

My 8-year-old son came home from school with a stuffed animal he had won at the class Valentine party.

"How did that happen?" I asked.

"Well," he explained, "the teacher put all our names together, and then picked one out.

"I cheated, though," he said looking guilty. "I prayed!"

—Davy Troxel
*(Intercession, Rewards)*

Dates used:_____

My 4-year-old daughter and I would always pray before she went to sleep. One night she volunteered to pray. She prayed and prayed and prayed—her voice getting softer and softer and softer, until only her lips were moving. Then she said "Amen."

"Honey," I said, "I didn't hear a word you said."

She answered, "Mama, I wasn't talking to you."

—Helen B. Poole
*(Eavesdropping, Intercession)*

Dates used:_____

A Sunday school teacher came to me with a picture depicting Christ in agonizing prayer in Gethsemane while his disciples slept in the background.

"I showed this picture to my class today," she announced, "and one of the students said, 'That reminds me of Pastor Winger.' "

Naturally, I was quite overwhelmed. While searching for an appropriate comment, I must have failed to catch the twinkle in the teacher's eyes. After I stammered a moment, she asked, "Want to know why this picture reminded my students of you?"

"Yes, of course," I said, trying to sound suitably humble.

"Well, Ronnie pointed to the sleeping disciples and said, 'You see, Jesus was praying so long, just like Pastor Winger does, that the disciples fell asleep!' "

—Walter Winger
*(Boredom, Patience)*

Dates used:_____

## Preachers

One day I sat down with my daughter and explained with pride that her grandfather was a preacher, her great-great grandfather was a preacher, and her great-great-great grandfather was a preacher. To which she replied, "Wow! We sure come from a long line of grandfathers."

—Linda Click
*(Grandparents, Heritage)*

Dates used:_____

## Pride

With reluctance, my grandson agreed to let his wife sell some of his old ties and suits in her yard sale. He thought they were fine, but she insisted they were outdated.

One shopper came by, picked up one of the old ties and a suit, and exclaimed, "Perfect!"

My grandson quickly gave his wife his wife a smug look—until the woman continued, "These will look terrific on my scarecrow!"

—Clara Null
*(Appearance, Humility)*

Dates used:_____

"It's showtime, baby!"

—Rob Portlock
*(Servanthood, Ushers)*

Dates used:_____

# Prophecy

Don't believe the "gloom and doom" experts who want to tell us about the future. Here are a three examples of bad predictions:

"A Japanese attack on Pearl Harbor is a strategic impossibility"

(George Fielding Eliot, 1938).

"Television won't be able to hold on to any market it captures after the first six months. People will soon get tired of staring at a plywood box every night"

(Darryl F. Zanuck, head of 20th-Century-Fox, 1946).

"Landing and moving around on the moon offers so many serious problems for human beings that it may take science another 200 years to lick them"

(Science Digest, August 1948).

*(Future, Predictions)*

Dates used:_____

Noted in a newspaper personal ad:

"Yesterday in this space I predicted that the world would come to an end. It did not, however. I regret any inconvenience this may have caused."

*(End Times, Future)*

Dates used:_____

## Punishment

An irate father phoned the Sunday school superintendent after his daughter had been attending a few weeks. "Our preschooler tells me if she misses Sunday school too often, you'll pitch her into the furnace! What in the world are you teaching in that church?"

Investigating the matter, the superintendent questioned the teacher. At first stumped, they finally put two-and-two together: stressing the importance of regular attendance on Sundays, the teacher had told her class that if they missed four consecutive weeks, they would be dropped from the register.

—*Christian Reader*
*(Confusion, Sunday School)*

Dates used:_____

# Relationships

No healthy person would want the neglect I
have to offer.

—comedian Jerry Seinfeld
*(Marriage, Neglect)*

Dates used:_____


My neighbor's son, Robert, seemed young to
be an usher at a wedding, but he was quickly
coached in wedding protocol. A veteran usher
instructed Robert to ask the person he was
escorting, "Are you a guest of the bride or
groom?" to know where to seat them.

Imagine our surprise when we heard Robert
ask, as he graciously offered his arm to the first
arrival, "Madam, whose side are you on?"

—Richard Blake
*(Ushers, Weddings)*

Dates used:_____

# Renewal

My family had gathered at my house for our yearly reunion. While we were in church singing the opening hymn, an earthquake hit. The building shook, and the overhead lights swung back and forth. In true California style we never missed a beat, even though we had to grab the pews in front to steady ourselves.

Following the service, the pastor came over to greet my out-of-town relatives. My son-in-law grinned as he shook the pastor's hand and said, "I've been to a lot of church services in my life, but I can honestly say this was the most moving one I've ever attended."

—June Cerza Kolf
*(Holy Spirit, Revival)*

Dates used:_____

The church was beautifully decorated for Christmas: poinsettias, evergreen boughs, golden bows, and a candle on the sill of each stained-glass window. Amid the beauty, the choir was presenting its cantata.

I wanted to capture this special event, so I asked a fellow churchgoer to videotape the service. He was happy to oblige and after experimenting decided the best place to set up was by the windows.

About fifteen minutes into the service, the cameraman leaned too close to the lit candle on the window sill, and his suit coat caught fire! Two alert folks hastily snuffed out the blaze. We rejoiced that no one was injured, and, as our minister of music quickly noted, "Finally, somebody was truly on fire for Jesus!"

—Tony Foeller
*(Christmas, Revival)*

Dates used:_____

# Repentance

When I was a telephone operator, a customer talked overtime on a long-distance call from a pay telephone booth. Even with my friendly reminders, he refused to deposit his overtime coins. Instead, he slammed down the phone, irate and verbally abusive.

A few seconds later, he was back on my line—somewhat calmer.

"Operator, please let me out of the phone booth—I'll pay, I'll pay, just let me out!"

The customer mistakenly thought I had control of the phone booth's doors and had locked him in! He gladly paid the overtime charge and with my advice gave the booth door a hefty kick to free himself.

—Lillian Pearsall
*(Atonement, Sin)*

Dates used:_____

## Resourcefulness

While shopping with my eight-year-old, he spotted a toy he wanted but didn't have enough money to buy. Since I wanted to teach him financial responsibility, I told him I couldn't give him the extra money.

In a brilliant display of resourcefulness, he reached into his mouth and, to the astonishment of onlookers, pulled out a loose baby tooth and handed it to me.

He got his toy.

—Donna McLean
*(Money, Responsibility)*

Dates used:_____

## Retirement

One woman's definition of retirement: "Twice the husband at half the salary."

*(Marriage, Work)*

Dates used:_____

## Revenge

My friend's four boys were young and bursting with energy, especially in church. But the sermon her minister preached on turning the other cheek got their undivided attention. The minister stressed that no matter what others do to us, we should never try to get even. That afternoon the youngest boy came into the house crying. Between sobs he told his mother he had kicked one of his brothers, who had kicked him in return.

"I'm sorry that you're hurt," his mother said. "But you shouldn't go around kicking people."

The tearful child replied, "But the preacher said he wasn't supposed to kick me back."

—Jane Vajnar
*(Arguments, Relationships)*

Dates used:_____

—Andy Robertson
*(Rest, Worship)*

Dates used:_____

## Sacrifice

Our seven-year-old daughter had just won $2 for her memory work in Sunday school. After the morning service, the pastor's wife congratulated her.

Our daughter proudly announced, "And I put it all in the morning's offering!"

"My, how wonderful!" the pastor's wife exclaimed. "I'm sure God will be pleased."

"Yes," the child replied, "now maybe God will let me do some of the things I want to do!"

—Genia Obal
*(Expectations, Giving)*

Dates used:_____

My seven-year-old daughter wanted to take violin lessons, so I took her to a music store to rent an instrument. Hoping she would understand the importance of making a commitment to practice, I explained to her that the lessons were expensive. I was willing to make the financial sacrifices if she promised to work hard. "There may be times you'll feel like giving up," I said, "but I want you to hang in there and keep on trying."

She nodded in understanding and then in her most serious voice said, "It will be just like marriage, right Mom?"

—Debra K. Johnson
*(Commitment, Marriage)*

Dates used:_____

## Scripture

The youth in my church had been studying the Book of Esther. I knew my son had been paying attention when we had brussels sprouts for supper. Spearing one and looking at it distastefully, he placed it in his mouth, saying, "If I perish, I perish."

—Frankie Roland
*(Courage, Fate)*

Dates used:_____

## Self-Esteem

I like talking to myself because I like dealing with a better class of people.

— comedian Jackie Mason
*(Pride, Smugness)*

Dates used:_____

"I don't know, Pastor, maybe it's an identity crisis.
I just can't seem to shake this feeling that I'm nothing …
a nobody, just an anonymous speck of dust on
this huge planet. I feel totally forgettable."

—Jonny Hawkins
*(Anonymity, Counseling)*

Dates used:_____

## Servanthood

My great-great uncle lived to the ripe old age of 106. He was healthy and spry and took joy in chauffering his less able-bodied senior friends around town. On his 100th birthday, his driver's license came up for renewal. When he went to the licensing bureau, the skeptical clerk said, "You're 100 years old! What do you need a driver's license for?"

My uncle, completely nonplussed, replied, "Somebody has to drive the old folks around!"

He continued to have a legal driver's license for the next five years.

—Barbara Klassen
*(Aging, Attitude)*

Dates used:_____

# Sharing

Four-year-old Sarah was invited to her first wedding, and she had lots of questions. At the reception, we explained there were two cakes—a groom's cake and a bride's cake.

"What's the matter, Mom," Sarah asked, "haven't they learned to share yet?"

—Patti Culver
*(Marriage, Weddings)*

Dates used:_____

My three-year-old grandson found a quarter in the driveway as the family left for church. When they returned home, he pulled it out of his pocket and handed it to his mother.

"You can have this money, Mommy. I was going to give it to Jesus, but he wasn't there."

—Joyce Parson
*(Giving, Worship)*

Dates used:_____

My grandchild was excited about his parents buying a new home with three bedrooms. He would have his own bedroom for the first time. But he surprised the real estate agent when he blurted, "It's too bad you don't have a house with another bedroom so Mom and Dad don't have to keep sharing a bedroom, too."

—Clara Null
*(Family, Marriage)*

Dates used:_____

# Sin

After telling a class of four- to seven-year-olds the story of Adam and Eve, I began to quiz them. "What was Eve's punishment for disobeying God?" I asked.

A bright-eyed girl raised her hand. "She had to crawl on her belly and eat dirt for the rest of her life."

—Ellen Cowan
*(Disobedience, Women)*

Dates used:_____


I had just finished a lesson on Christian behavior. "Now, Billy," I asked, "tell me what we must do before we can expect to be forgiven for our sins."

Without hesitation, Billy replied, "First we gotta sin."

—Clara Null
*(Forgiveness, Repentance)*

Dates used:_____

# Who's Afraid of the
# **Small Home Group?**

## Are you one of the many with ill-founded fears of. . .

## Sports

In a never-ending effort to attract the unchurched, some churches have considered translating their unfamiliar terminology into familiar football phrases. Although these definitions are not the best football and certainly not the best theology, they would help initiate football fans into the complexities of church life.

*Blocking:* Talking endlessly to the pastor at the church door and keeping everyone else from exiting.

*Draft choice:* The decision to sit close to an air-conditioning vent.

*Draw play:* What restless children do during a long sermon.

*End around:* Diaper-changing time in the nursery.

*End zone:* The pews.

*Extra point:* What you receive when you tell the preacher his sermon was too short.

*Face mask:* Smiling and saying everything is fine when it isn't.

*Forward motion:* The invitation at an evangelistic service.

*Fullback:* What the choir sees while the sermon is delivered.

*Halfback:* What the organist sees.

*Hash marks:* Stains left on the tablecloth after a potluck.                    *(continued)*

*Head linesman:* The one who changes the overhead projector transparencies.

*Illegal use of hands:* Clapping at an inappropriate point in the service.

*Illegal motion:* Leaving before the benediction.

*In the pocket:* Where some church members keep God's tithe.

*Incomplete pass:* A dropped offering plate.

*Interference:* Talking during the prelude.

*Linebacker:* A statistic used by a preacher to support a point just made.

*Passing game:* The maneuver required of latecomers when the person sitting at the end of the pew won't slide to the middle.

*Quarterback:* What tightwads want after putting fifty cents in the offering.

*Running backs:* Those who make repeated trips to the rest room.

*Through the uprights:* Getting things done via the elders or church board.

*Touchback:* The laying on of hands.

*Two-minute warning:* The chairman of the board looking at his watch in full view of the preacher.

—William Ellis
*(Assimilation, Church)*

Dates used:_____

## Stewardship

Paul Harvey's broadcast (11/22/95) shared this insight.

The Butter Ball Turkey Company set up a hot line to answer consumer questions about preparing holiday turkeys. One woman called to inquire about cooking a turkey that had been in her freezer for twenty-three years! The operator told her it might be safe if the freezer had been kept below 0 degrees the entire time. But the operator warned the woman that, even if it were safe, the flavor had probably deteriorated, and she wouldn't recommend eating it.

The caller replied, "That's what we thought. We'll just give it to the church."

—Rik Danielson
*(Generosity, Stinginess)*

Dates used:_____

## Stress

I was wearing a T-shirt with the words: Be nice to me. I had a hard day. Little Eric looked at the words and said, "How can you tell this early in the morning?"

—Verna Chambers
*(Expectations, Foresight)*

Dates used:_____

My friend Dorothy spent several weeks in prayer and special training to lead a Bible discussion group. Finally the big day arrived for the first class. Getting her family of six out the door was more hectic than usual that morning. Breakfast didn't turn out right, and several arguments were going on among the children. Dorothy, quickly getting frazzled, tried to regain her composure. In the midst of the bedlam, her husband entered the kitchen and surveyed the uproar.

"Kids! Settle down!" he admonished. "Your mom has only 45 minutes until she has to become a radiant Christian."

—Roseann Hill
*(Example, Lifestyle)*

Dates used:_____

Chippie the parakeet never saw it coming. One second he was peacefully perched in his cage singing, the next he was sucked in, washed up, and blown over.

His problem began when his owner decided to clean his cage with a vacuum. She stuck the nozzle in to suck up the seeds and feathers in the bottom of the cage. Then the phone rang. Instinctively she turned to pick it up. She barely said hello when—sswwwwwppppp! Chippie got sucked in. She gasped, let the phone drop, and snapped off the vacuum. With her heart in her mouth, she unzipped the bag.

There was Chippie—alive, but stunned—covered with heavy black dust. She grabbed him and rushed to the bathtub, turned on the faucet full blast, and held Chippie under a torrent of ice-cold water, power-washing him clean. So she did what any compassionate pet owner would do: she snatched up the hair dryer and blasted the wet, shivering little bird with hot air.

Chippie doesn't sing much anymore.

—Chuck Swindoll
*(Depression, Trials)*

Dates used:_____

"I, too, was saved from a life of addictions.
I was hooked on phonics."

—Jonny Hawkins
*(Addictions, Salvation)*

Dates used:_____

163

# Tactfulness

The elderly pastor's wife was known for her ability to make positive comments about every facet of her husband's ministry. The church choir, however, consisting of seniors in their seventies and eighties, had defied positive but truthful comment.

She finally solved the problem one Sunday morning. As the choir members filed into the choir loft, she leaned over and remarked, "Aren't they walking well this morning?"

—Anne Phillips
*(Criticism, Diplomacy)*

Dates used:_____

As a lady in our church was singing a solo, my four-year-old grandson tugged at my sleeve. "Nana," he said, "she can't sing very well, can she?"

Knowing the deep faith of this wonderful lady, I said, "Chandler, she sings from her heart, so it's good." He nodded with understanding.

Several days later as we were singing along with the car radio, Chandler interrupted me. "Nana," he said, "you sing from your heart too, don't you?"

—Barbara McKeever
*(Criticism, Diplomacy)*

Dates used:_____

In *Be a People Person,* John Maxwell tells this story:

Mr. Myrick had to go to Chicago on business and persuaded his brother to take care of his cat during his absence. Though he hated cats, the brother agreed. Upon his return, Myrick called from the airport to check on the cat.

"Your cat died," the brother reported, then hung up.

Myrick was inconsolable. His grief was magnified by his brother's insensitivity, so he called again to express his pain. "There was no need for you to be so blunt," he said.

"What was I supposed to say?" asked the perplexed brother.

"You could have broken the news gradually," explained Myrick. "You could have said, 'The cat was playing on the roof.' Then, later in the conversation, you could have said, 'He fell off.' Then you could have said, 'He broke his leg.' Then when I came to pick him up, you could have said, 'I'm so sorry. Your cat passed away during the night.' You've got to learn to be more tactful.

"By the way, how's Mom?"

After a long pause, the brother replied, "She's playing on the roof."

—Mike Neifert
*(Criticism, Diplomacy)*

Dates used:_____

166

## Ten Commandments

My Sunday school class of first graders were learning the Ten Commandments. When we got to "Thou shalt not commit adultery," I wondered if I would have to explain this to them.

Sure enough, suddenly a seven-year-old girl raised her hand and asked, "What does *commit* mean?"

—Clara Null
*(Adultery, Sunday School)*

Dates used:_____

A third-grade Sunday school teacher was giving a lesson on the commandment, "Honor thy father and mother."

"Now, does anyone know a commandment for brothers and sisters?" she asked.

One sharp girl raised her hand and said, "Thou shalt not kill."

—Jack Seberry
*(Murder, Parents)*

Dates used:_____

A fourth-grade Sunday school completed several lessons on the Ten Commandments by asking the kids, "What is the hardest commandment for you to keep?"

Most responded, "Thou shalt not commit adultery."

She couldn't understand why fourth graders would find that command a problem until a mother quizzed her son on what he meant. Without blinking, the boy replied, "Thou shalt not sass back to adults."

—Sheryl Tedder
*(Adultery, Sin)*

Dates used:_____

While working as the chaplain for the Cub Scouts, I conducted a vesper service at each meeting. One evening the lesson was on the Ten Commandments, so I asked the kids if they could name any. They began to call out a number of them, including, "Don't drink and drive."

—James Isenberg
*(Alcohol, Sin)*

Dates used:_____

Compliments You're Not Sure You Want to Hear When Preaching a Series on the Ten Commandments:

1. Thou shalt have no other gods before me. *"A simply divine sermon, Pastor."*

2. Thou shalt make no graven images. *"You illustrated perfectly what God really looks like."*

3. Thou shalt not take the Lord's name in vain. *"As God is my judge, that was your best sermon ever."*

4. Remember the sabbath, to keep it holy. *"Excellent bit of work, Pastor."*

5. Honor thy father and mother. *"Wish my dad could hear you preach—he could sure use it."*

6. Thou shalt not kill. *"Anyone who slept through that one ought to be shot."*

7. Thou shalt not commit adultery. *"Glad you don't intrude into other people's affairs."*

8. Thou shalt not steal. *"Good sermon, Reverend—you preach it better than Schuller did on TV last week."*

9. Thou shalt not bear false witness. *"I'm literally in heaven when I hear you preach, Pastor."*

10. Thou shalt not covet. *"I really envy your ability to speak well in public."*

—David Landegent
*(Compliments, Praise)*

Dates used:_____

# Thankfulness

One Sunday in church, members were praising the Lord for what he had done in their lives that week. Mr. Segault said that the roof of his house had caught on fire, but fortunately, a neighbor had seen it, and the possible disaster was averted with only minor damage.

A minute later, a woman stood up. "I have a praise, too," she said. "I'm Mr. Segault's insurance agent."

—Ariana Macksey
*(Church, Community)*

Dates used:_____

# Theology

A new members' class gave some new definitions to theological jargon.

*Old nature.* Last year's leaves.

*Sanctification.* What happened to the boat on vacation.

*Discipleship.* A boat belonging to Peter.

*Total Commitment.* A covenant to eat one type of breakfast cereal.

—Eutychus in *Christianity Today*
*(Insight, Understanding)*

Dates used:_____

## Thrift

Ronald Warwick, captain of the luxury cruise ship *Queen Elizabeth II,* questioned a passenger who paid full fare for his dog to join them on an around-the-world cruise. (Accommodations range from $25,000 to $150,000.) "Wouldn't it have cost less to leave him at home?"

"Oh no," the man said. "When we are away a long time, the dog's psychiatrist fees are so high, it's less expensive to bring him along."

—*USA Today* (10/25/95)
*(Extravagance, Priorities)*

Dates used:_____

## Tithing

My five-year-old son was proud of the fact he had graduated from bow ties to a necktie just like Dad's. But one Sunday morning, with his hand clutching the tie tightly, I heard this panicked whisper: "Dad, why did the pastor say they're going to collect the ties and offering?"

—G. Brian Manning
*(Giving, Sacrifice)*

Dates used:_____

Unlike the IRS, the church has always kept its requirements simple: a straight 10 percent off the top. But perhaps church officials should consider engaging in some "Tithe Reform."

The new T-4, Estimated Tithe Declaration Forms, could work like this: On line 1, write down the amount of your regular paycheck. On line 2, enter the number of times you go to church each year. Multiply the number on line 2 by 3.056. Enter the result on line 3. On line 4 enter your age when you first professed Christ. On line 5, enter your pastor's salary. (This can be found on the photcopied budget distributed at your church's annual meeting, which is always held on the day of the Super Bowl.)

Compare line 5 with line 1. Feel guilty. Subtract line 5 from line 1. Take a deep breath and ignore the result. Multiply the amount on line 1 by .10 and enter it on line 6. Throw in a few extra bucks to make you feel better about the minister's salary. And write that check.

—Eutychus in *Christianity Today*
*(Generosity, Taxes)*

Dates used:_____

172

## Trust

Travel is hard enough without the airline industry scaring us with their terminology.

As I drive to the airport, watching for the signs that indicate what exits to take, I wonder what sadist named the place where you trust your all to a creaking bunch of nuts and bolts, *Terminal*.

When I check in at the counter, I remember this particular flight was chosen by my travel agent for one reason—it was *the cheapest available.*

When it's time to land, why does the flight attendant have to remind us that we are making *our final approach?* (On a recent flight, the attendant announced reassuringly, "We will be *in* the ground very shortly.")

When the flight attendant warns us not to move until the plane has reached a *complete stop,* I wonder what an incomplete stop would be like.

—Leonard Sweet
*(Fear, Travel)*

Dates used:_____

## Uncertainty

Some questions we'll probably never have answered this side of heaven.

Why isn't *phonetic* spelled the way it sounds?

Why are there interstate highways in Hawaii?

Why are there flotation devices under plane seats, instead of parachutes?

Why are cigarettes sold in gas stations when smoking is prohibited there?

Have you ever imagined a world with no hypothetical situations?

How does the guy who drives the snowplow get to work in the morning?

If 7-Eleven is open 24 hours a day, 365 days a year, why are there locks on the doors?

If nothing ever sticks to Teflon, how do they make Teflon stick to the pan?

Why do we drive on parkways and park on driveways?

Why is it when you transport something by car, it's called a *shipment,* but when you transport something by ship, it's called *cargo?*

*(Curiosity, God's Omniscience)*

Dates used:_____

## Unhappiness

Ten Commandments for an Unhappy Life.

1. Thou shalt wear a grim expression at all times, and thou shalt hold thy body in a stiff and rigid posture, and exercise thy muscles as little as possible.

2. Thou shalt never get too close to anybody.

3. Thou shalt stuff and store all thy feeling in thy gut.

4. Thou shalt put aside play, and shalt inflict upon others that which was once inflicted upon thyself.

5. Thou shalt remain logical and analytical whenever possible.

6. Thou shalt go to as many "all-you-can-eat" buffets as thou canst.

7. Thou shalt not party.

8. Thou shalt not take a vacation.

9. Thou shalt expect the worst in all situations, blame and shame everyone around thyself for everything, and dwell on the feebleness, faults, and fears of others.

10. Thou shalt be in control at all times, no matter what.

—Leonard Sweet
*(Health, Stress)*

Dates used:_____

# Unity

Weddings in our church always included the lighting of a unity candle. At one rehearsal I was explaining the symbolism of the candle ceremony.

"After the middle candle is lit, blowing out the two side candles means the two become one," I said.

"Oh," a guest admitted in surprise. "I always thought it meant 'no more flames.'"

—Greg Asimakoupoulos
*(Marriage, Weddings)*

Dates used:_____

## Ushers

The Top 10 Reasons It's Great to Be an Usher.

10. You get to wear a badge.

9. You don't have to sit on a hard pew for the whole service.

8. You can slip out to the restroom if you need to, and nobody notices.

7. You get to tell people where to go.

6. You get to take money from people.

5. You don't have to be as friendly as the greeters.

4. You get to eat a lot of breath mints.

3. If a screaming child bothers you, you can do something about it.

2. Preachers preach to the choir, not to the ushers.

1. You get to seat latecomers in the front row.

—Jerry Beres, Russell Snyder
*(Volunteers, Worship)*

Dates used:_____

# Vision

A golfer's errant shot ended up on an ant hill. He squared up, took a big swing—and missed. Thousands of innocent ants were killed. The hacker took another swing—and missed again. Another wave of ants was destroyed. Panic-stricken insects scurried everywhere.

One ant finally took charge. "Follow me," he cried with authority. Another ant yelled, "But where are we going?"

He pointed to the golf ball sitting in front of them. "There. If we don't get on the ball, we're going to die!"

*(Leadership, Mistakes)*

Dates used:_____

"It was safe to say that Pastor Mel's
vision statement hadn't yet caught fire."

—Steve Phelps
(Boards, Enthusiasm)

Dates used:_____

"I'm sorry, could you repeat that?
I didn't catch the first four words."

—Tim Liston
*(Communication, Listening)*

Dates used:_____

181

# Weddings

At a wedding, my granddaughter Melissa asked, "Why is a bride always dressed in white?"

"Because white represents happiness, and today is the happiest day of her life," I replied.

Her next question was: "Then why is the groom dressed in black?"

—Clara Null
*(Happiness, Marriage)*

Dates used:_____


I was watching my five-year-old granddaughter play with her toys. At one point, she staged a wedding, first playing the role of the mother who assigned specific duties, then suddenly becoming the bride with her "teddy bear" groom.

She picked him up and said to the "minister" presiding over the wedding, "Now you can read us our rights."

Without missing a beat, she became the minister who said, "You have the right to remain silent, anything you say may be held against you, you have the right to have an attorney present. You may kiss the bride."

—Sonja Ely
*(Happiness, Rights)*

Dates used:_____

Former Education Secretary William Bennett recently attended a contemporary wedding where the bride and groom pledged, in their wedding vows, to remain together, "as long as love shall last."

"I sent paper plates as my wedding gift," Bennett said.

*—The Detroit News*
*(Commitment, Marriage)*

Dates used:_____

# Weight

Medical surveys indicate that 60 percent of Americans are overweight. Of course, those are just round figures.

*(Fitness, Health)*

Dates used:_____

## Work

A TV weather reporter lost her job because her forecasts were never accurate. In an interview for another position, she was asked why she left her last job.

"The climate didn't agree with me," she replied.

*(Excuses, Honesty)*

Dates used:_____

## Worry

Rick Majerus, men's basketball coach at the University of Utah, recently captured a common concern:

"Everyone's worried about the economy this year. Hey, my hairline is in recession, my waistline is in inflation, and altogether, I'm in depression."

—*The Arizona Republic*
*(Aging, Economy)*

Dates used:_____

# Worship

A woman entered a Häagen-Dazs store on the Kansas City Plaza for an ice-cream cone. After making her selection, she turned and found herself face to face with Paul Newman, in town filming the movie *Mr. & Mrs. Bridge.* He smiled and said hello. Newman's blue eyes caused her knees to shake.

She managed to pay for her cone, then left the shop, heart pounding. When she gained her composure, she realized she didn't have her snack. She started back into the store to get it and met Newman at the door.

"Are you looking for your ice cream?" he asked. She nodded, unable to speak. "You put it in your purse with your change."

When was the last time the presence of God quickened our pulse?

—*The Kansas City Star*
*(Embarrassment, Idols)*

Dates used:_____

Sniglets are words that don't appear in the dictionary, but should. Here are a few words to broaden your worship vocabulary.

*Boiked*—What an usher feels after going out of his way to take an offering plate to someone alone in a pew, and the person has nothing to contribute.

*Pliturgist*—The man or woman who is alway half a second ahead of the rest of the congregation during a responsive reading.

*Jobbling*—The gradual rising of the congregation during the final hymn, after the pastor has forgotten to say, "Please rise."

*Pleech*—A joyful congregant's first note of verse four, when the bulletin said to stop after three.

*Scruggles*—The scattered, congregational coughs that follow inevitably after someone gets them started.

*Grooncher*—A 240-pound greeter who thinks his job is to crush hands, not shake them.

*Scriggling*— The act of wasting one's time thinking up Christian sniglets.

—Eutychus in *Christianity Today*
*(Choirs, Ushers)*

Dates used:_____

# Youth

A recent on-line discussion followed the question, *Is it appropriate for girls to ask guys out for dates?* One teenage boy wrote, "It would be OK for a girl to ask me out. It would be surprising, but OK."

—*Campus Life's* Yakety Yak message board
*(Dating, Insecurity)*

Dates used:_____


Eighteen-year-old Jennifer Connor, a New York teen with a high hairdo, was diagnosed in 1989 with hearing loss and a "serious" ear infection. Her physician said her ears were clogged with hair spray.

—*Beyond News of the Weird*
by Chuck Shepherd, John J. Kohut & Roland Sweet
*(Beauty, Vanity)*

Dates used:_____

# Zeal

An unemployed executive answered an intriguing job ad for the regional zoo. The human resources manager explained that the zoo's gorilla had died, and it was cheaper to hire someone to dress in a gorilla's suit than to get another gorilla. The man was desperate for a job, so he took it.

The first day wasn't too bad. He paced the floor, ate the peanuts and bananas thrown to him, and thumped on his chest. The next day, he became bolder and began swinging on the rope tied to an old tree. As he swung, he suddenly lost his grip and fell into the lion's den next door.

He jumped to his feet and began to scream, "Help! Help!" The lion came out of his house to see what the noise was all about, then pounced on the man in the gorilla suit.

"Shhh! If you don't shut up, we'll both lose our jobs!"

*(Pretense, Workplace)*

Dates used:_____

## Pastor to Pastor

Let's face it. Your peers can be a tough audience. Women and men who communicate professionally hold a higher standard for one of their own.

That's why we've included this "Pastor to Pastor" section. When speaking to fellow pastors, whether at the local ministerial alliance or the big national conference, fresh humor is the quickest way to disarm your critics and energize your colleagues.

Here, from the archives of *Leadership,* are some of the funniest stories we've heard about life in the ministry.

## Bad Days

It's a bad day when . . .

• You call the groom by the bride's former boyfriend's name.

• Your personal parking spot gets relocated—to the Denny's Restaurant three blocks away.

• You forget to turn off the cordless microphone while using the rest room.

• The church begins exploring the possibility of a missionary trip for you—to Libya.

• The organist is asked to play while you preach.

• The church votes to change your day off to Sunday.

• You preach the same sermon for the second week—and nobody notices.

• You get assigned to nursery duty—during the morning service.

—Bruce Hoppe, Dwight Dally, Dave Maurer, Ron Saari
*(Discouragement, Mistakes)*

Dates used:_____

You know you're having *another* bad day when. . .

• You finally remember the name of that person you promised to visit in the hospital—while reading the obituaries.

• The groundskeeper accidentally waters your study along with the flower bed.

• You can't find Obadiah while leading a Bible study.

• In the pulpit you notice your sermon notes this week are for last week's sermon.

• The youth pastor urgently asks you about the church's liability insurance.

• Your church treasurer sends you a postcard from Geneva.

• The manse redecoration committee gets 'a great deal' on used chartreuse carpet.

• You are informed that the youth group used steel wool sponges for their car wash.

• The couple you married a year ago calls to ask about a warranty.

• You are elected pastor emeritus—and you're only 28.

—James D. Berkley
*(Discouragement, Mistakes)*

Dates used:_____

You know you're having *yet another bad day when* . . .

- You're the only one at the potluck dinner.
- You ask your secretary to "Take a letter" and she chooses *Q*.
- Before the annual meeting, the church treasurer asks if you know of a copier that copies in red.
- A church in Haiti wants to send its youth group to renovate your building.
- The city designates the next-door lot as a landfill site.

—Dave Veerman
*(Church, Trials)*

Dates used:_____

"Where's my husband this morning?
Right where you buried him last week."

—Mary Chambers
*(Funerals, Mistakes)*

Dates used:_____

## Church Planting

You know you're in church planting when ...

• A baby sneezes in the nursery, and the mother leaves the service to check his health.

• You discover you've preached three sermons in the past month on "Commitment and Faithfulness through Church Attendance."

• Your spouse is ill—and attendance dips 20 percent.

• Your hymnals (copyright 1895), your pulpit (ninth-grade shop quality), your (dented) Communion set, and your core members are all castoffs from Old First Church.

• Your attendance matches the temperature —in January.

• Soloists always use taped accompaniment.

• Your first visitor in two months comes on the Sunday three families are gone—and you're preaching on tithing.

• Your services, held in a hotel conference room, are interrupted by passers-by looking for the Baseball Card and Comic Book Convention.

• You find the three missing families at the convention.

• Anything that breathes is counted in Sunday attendance.

• Your donated organ has built-in percussion for the rhumba and cha-cha.

*(continued)*

• Your favorite Bible verse is "Where two or three are gathered together ..."

• You say, "Will the usher please come forward."

• You awake from a dream in which everyone who has ever visited your church comes back.

• The phone number of the church and parsonage are the same.

• A board member asks, "Why do we need a budget?"

• Every piece of furniture has to be put away after the service.

• Even buckets of air freshener on Sundays cannot remove the smell of smoke and sweat remaining in the rented sanctuary from the other six days.

• You need to speak to the church chairman, Sunday school superintendent, and treasurer—but he's gone this week.

• Infants can crawl from the nursery to the pulpit in 19.3 seconds.

—Rich Geigert
*(Humility, Small Church)*

Dates used:_____

# Church Talk

Sometimes the church seems to have a language of its own. While insiders understand it well, the uninitiated may not understand the subtle nuances of Churchese. Perhaps a glossary would help:

*Statement:* "We'll sing only the first verse of our closing hymn."
*Definition:* "I preached too long."

*Statement:* "It's VBS time again."
*Definition:* "Start saving Legg's containers, Popsicle sticks, egg cartons, and baby food jars."

*Statement:* "This is the best book I've read on the subject."
*Definition:* "This is the only book I've read on the subject."

*Statement:* "Everybody is saying …"
*Definition:* "My wife told me …"

*Statement:* "Our church is close-knit."
*Definition:* "We haven't had a new member in five years."

—David E. Steverson
*(Church, Discernment)*

Dates used:_____

The word *oxymoron* comes from the Greek words for "sharp fool." That's the only way to describe phrases like "jumbo shrimp," "deafening silence," and "freezer burn." You may have heard these oxymorons at church:

10. Board consensus
9. Creative worship
8. Brief treasurer's report
7. Work party
6. Junior high sleepover
5. Men's fellowship
4. Close-knit staff
3. Simple request
2. Bus ministry
1. My final point

—Ronald T. Habermas and Gary Habermas
*(Church, Confusion)*

Dates used:_____

## Computers

Here, for the terminologically impaired, are some handy definitions of commonly used computer terms.

*Shareware:* A common Communion chalice.

*Cyberspace:* Where people go when we preach on stuff like supralapsarianism.

*Hardware:* The ugly necktie your kids gave you last Father's Day.

*Download:* To dump unpleasant tasks on the youth pastor.

*Hard drive:* A twelve-hour bus trip to junior high camp.

*Co-processor:* When your wife edits your sermons.

*Modem:* What you did to the flowers Mrs. Grinch planted in front of the church.

*Database:* Old Mrs. Weemster who remembers the names and shortcomings of every pastor in the 120-year history of your church.

*PC:* "Please Come"—an eschatological plea by those who can't find their sermon notes on the computer when it's time to print them Sunday morning.

*Online:* Where your job will be when you step up to the pulpit with nothing to say.

—Ed Rowell
*(Church, Technology)*

Dates used:_____

## Counseling

Not every pastor enjoys counseling. But other than by skipping town, how can you decrease the demand? Here, based on specious clinical research, are a dozen methods guaranteed to keep counseling off your to-do list.

1.  Recite tales of people who are a lot worse off, and call the counselee a cry baby.
2.  Engage the counselee's mother-in-law as a co-therapist.
3.  Don't put a door on your office.
4.  Sing songs such as "Put On a Happy Face" and "Don't Worry; Be Happy" to counselees.
5.  Step out of the office and start laughing uproariously.
6.  Tell the counselee that although you can't figure out a solution to the problem, you'll bring it up in the sermon on Sunday and see if anybody has any ideas.
7.  Casually catch up on your reading while counselees bare their deepest problems.
8.  Tell the counselee you are videotaping the session for replay on the local cable program: "Candid Clergy."
9.  Put a bumper sticker on your car: I'D RATHER NOT BE COUNSELING.

*(continued)*

203

10. Refer them to a helpful article in your favorite professional journal: the *National Enquirer.*
11. Suggest counseling by fax machine.
12. In front of the counselee, phone your spouse and ask for his or her opinion on what to do.

—Paul Bailey
*(Hardheartedness, Pastoral Care)*

Dates used:_____

# Definitions

Have you ever noticed church phenomena for which there should be a term, yet none exists? No longer. Introducing ... *The Living Lexicon: Church Terms That Oughta Be.*

*Biblidue:* The build-up of bookmarks, bulletins, notes, and other miscellanea that collects in one's Bible.

*Clivaholic:* One who can no longer control the compulsion to quote C. S. Lewis in every sermon, lesson, or conversation.

*Hymnastics:* The entertaining body language of the song leader.

*Narthexegesis:* Unsolicited post-sermon commentary given the preacher by armchair biblical theologians.

*(continued)*

*Pewtrify:* To occupy a precise spot in the sanctuary for more than fifteen years without once showing signs of sentient life.

*Ministereotype:* A common myth or misconception about any ordained person.

*Pulpituitary:* That phenomenon familiar to those seated on the front pew, during which a preacher produces hazardous conditions with alliterative P's.

*Deaconscript:* An unwilling church officer cajoled into a position of leadership.

*Hi-litaholic:* One who cannot resist highlighting Bible verses until the entire volume is a multihued mass of Day-Glo vibrancy.

*Hymnprovisation:* The abrupt and unannounced transition from one song to another, usually a chorus unfamiliar to most present.

—Rob Suggs
*(Church, Discernment)*

Dates used:_____

A district superintendent often assists local churches in their search for new pastors. If the D.S. calls you as a potential candidate, the D.S. will try to give you a feel for the congregation. To help pastors translate these assessments, we submit the following list:

When the District Superintendent says, *"I just need someone to go in there and love the people."*

What the D.S. means is, This group is on the verge of a major church split.

*"This church simply needs an injection of new life."*

The senior adult class constitutes 90 percent of the membership.

*"There's a good core of young marrieds in the church."*

The young marrieds Sunday school class has been going for 42 years, and they haven't bothered to change their name.

*"This congregation has an involved, well-mobilized laity."*

They've demanded recall votes of the last six pastors.

*"With a little bit of time, this church could bust loose."*

The most cantankerous church boss is experiencing health problems and may die soon.

*(continued)*

206

*"This church offers a competitive salary package."*

It's on par with what the cashier at Wal-Mart makes.

*"This church features uplifting music."*

The organist is so bad she makes your hair stand on end.

*"The building is highly visible."*

The property is located so far off the beaten path that there's open space for miles around.

*"The leadership is very, very stable."*

The last time there was turnover on the church board was during the Eisenhower administration.

*"You won't believe the benefits."*

There are none.

*"I know you're the one for the job."*

Please take this assignment so I can spend more time on the golf course.

—Brad Edgbert, Joe Shreffler,

Scott Thornton, John Whitsett

*(Church, Discernment)*

Dates used:_____

## Exercise

Who says ministry is a sedentary occupation? Now you can keep track of the energy expended by such routine pastoral tasks as:

Jumping to conclusions—10 calories

Bending over backwards—25 calories

Bowing to pressure—25 calories

Climbing the walls—50 calories

Gnashing teeth—50 calories

Going the second mile—50 calories

Putting your hand to the plow—60 calories

Reaping what you sow—75 calories

Turning the other cheek—90 calories

Casting the first stone—90 calories

Throwing your weight around—50 to 300 calories (depending on your weight)

Making mountains out of molehills—150 calories

Moving mountains—200 calories

Digging into the Greek—110 calories

Eating crow—75 calories

Riding a hobby horse—20 calories

Pushing programs—300 calories

Bending an ear—60 calories

Casting pearls before swine—80 calories

Carrying the weight of the world—200 calories

Laying up treasure in heaven—250 calories

*(continued)*

Upholding the church in prayer—275
  calories
Talking to the board chairman—300 calories
Listening to the board chairman—2 calories

—Terry C. Muck, Dean Merrill, Marshall Shelley
*(Ministry, Pastoral Care)*

Dates used:_____

## Guest Speakers

You know you're in trouble when the guest speaker begins with ...

A funny thing happened on the way to the church this morning ...

Unaccustomed as I am to public speaking ...

Did you hear the one about the three ministers on an airplane ...

Here are the notes for the sermon I was going to give, but I've decided not to give that message and simply say some things that need to be said ...

As I was eating lunch with (insert big name) last week ...

Webster defines (insert any word) as ...

Yesterday's Cubs game has many parallels to this morning's text ...

My wife doesn't like this sermon, but I decided to go ahead with it anyway ...

This morning's message has twenty points ...

*(continued)*

Last night I had a dream—of footprints in the sand …

Cereal boxes don't usually lead to sermon ideas, but this morning …

There are some topics that thirty minutes just can't do justice …

I was digging through some old seminary class notes this week …

At first glance, variants between the Septuagint and the Masoretic Text don't seem all that interesting, but …

Over the last few months, while struggling with my sexual identity …

I normally prepare my sermons in advance, but today …

—Kevin A. Miller
*(Impressions, Preaching)*

Dates used:_____

## Good News

*Good News:* You baptized four people today.

*Bad News:* You lost two others in the swift river current.

*Good News:* The Women's Association voted to send you a get-well card.

*Bad News:* It passed 31 to 30.

*Good News:* The church board accepted your job description the way you wrote it.

*(continued)*

*Bad News:* They also formed a search committee to find somebody capable of filling the position.

*Good News:* Your stand on nuclear disarmament has won the respect and admiration of many people.

*Bad News:* None of them is remotely connected to your church.

*Good News:* You finally found a choir director who approaches things your way.

*Bad News:* The choir mutinied.

*Good News:* Seventy junior high students showed up last Thursday.

*Bad News:* The meeting was on Wednesday.

*Good News:* Your women's softball team won their first game.

*Bad News:* They beat your men's softball team.

*Good News:* The trustees finally voted to add more church parking.

*Bad News:* They want to blacktop the front lawn of the manse.

—James D. Berkley
*(Disappointment, Perspective)*

Dates used:_____

## Illustrations

A Pastor's Top Ten Favorite Illustrations

10. Someone else's big mistake.
 9. The bumper sticker I read on the way to church.
 8. My last vacation.
 7. My kid's darling, off-the-cuff remark.
 6. Anything from *Reader's Digest* found while waiting for the doctor.
 5. An old joke, which magically becomes "something that happened to a friend of mine."
 4. The story of my only fishing trip, made to sound like an *National Geographic* expedition.
 3. The day I won "the big game."
 2. The day I lost "the big game."
 1. The day I finally told the truth about "the big game."

—Michael E. Phillips
*(Jokes, Stories)*

Dates used:_____

## Last Words

Here are the most frequent phrases in ministry that become preludes to a fast farewell.

10. I think I've earned the right to say this.

9. Thank you for the unanimous vote of confidence.

8. We'll incorporate a seeker-sensitive approach into our present worship service.

7. In ancient Israel, the people *danced* before the Lord.

6. Recently, I've been reading about the importance of publicly confessing your own sins, so today ...

5. I'll show the church secretary who's boss around here!

4. I'm sure I can trust you to keep this confidential.

3. Then there are no hard feelings, right?

2. I'm sure Mrs. Jones will agree that she's been our organist long enough.

1. They need to realize this kitchen belongs to everyone.

—Bob Moeller and the LEADERSHIP editors
*(Conflict, Leadership)*

Dates used:_____

## Prayer

I pastor a young church that still meets in temporary facilities. During the usual chaos of setting up for worship, I heard one of my parishioners complain about back pain. Just before the service, his wife explained that Jack was recovering from surgery.

During the pastoral prayer, Jack's name came to mind. I asked God to help him recover from surgery and to "restore him to full function." I heard a gasp and some muffled laughter.

I found out after the service that Jack's surgery was a vasectomy.

—Mike Coglan
*(Embarrassment, Pastoral Care)*

Dates used:_____

# Pulpit Committees

It's important to read between the lines of what the pulpit committee says, so you know what it really means.

*When the pulpit committee says, "Our church is in a delightful rural setting."*

No visitors will ever find it.

*"The parsonage is conveniently located to the church."*

It's right next door, so you'll never have a moment's quiet.

*"We have 246 members on the roll."*

Sunday morning worship attendance is 20.

*"We want to reach the unchurched in our area."*

We want a pastor who will evangelize for us.

*"Church members are active in community affairs."*

Good luck finding volunteers to teach Sunday school.

*"We're seeking someone to revitalize the church."*

The church needs to be painted.

*"We'll be glad to review your performance periodically."*

You can expect to get a phone call every Sunday afternoon.

*"We'd like a hard-working pastor."*

*(continued)*

You get one day off a month.

*"We want to build a strong youth program."*

Our last addition to the cradle roll was in 1959.

*"We'd like our pastor to be a family person."*

We hope your children can help set up chairs and your spouse can type the bulletin.

—Jack and Ann Wald
*(Expectations, Honesty)*

Dates used:_____

## Resumes

Have you ever wondered why your pastoral resume doesn't evoke more enthusiasm? Here, as a public service, are some statements you might want to edit out of your next resume.

"I believe empathy is overrated."

"In the five churches I have faithfully served over the past two years . . ."

"My hobbies are pit bulls and automatic weapons."

"I am willing to sacrifice my family for the sake of the ministry. I am also willing to sacrifice yours."

"I have learned to cope with financial crisis at every church I've served."

"I require an attractive secretary and/or organist."

"My extensive counseling of church members has proved a rich source of sermon illustrations."

"I've been told that every sermon I preach is better than the next."

"My personality has provided me ample opportunity to develop conflict-resolution skills."

—Dave Wilkinson
*(Disclosure, Perspective)*

Dates used:_____

**SERVICE**

"And never, ever look at serving
the church as burdensome."

—Jonny Hawkins
*(Bondage, Obligation)*

Dates used:_____

## Spiritual Gifts

Seven True Spiritual Gifts for Today's Church:

1. *Nursery worker.* This is based on Mark 10:14, "Suffer the little children to come to me." Anyone who believes this verse is or should be in the Bible has nursery-worker for his or her dominant gift.

2. *Giving.* This is the dominant gift for anybody who makes more money than I do. Michael Jordan, for example, would fit in this category if he came to my church. In fact, he's thinking about coming to my church, so he's asked me to tell everybody else's church to get off his back about it.

3. *Criticism.* Although not actually mentioned in the text, this is in fact the most widely practiced spiritual gift in the church today, so the academy has finally voted that it be officially recognized.

4. *Amway.* Discretion forbids me to say more.

5. *Wedding Hostess.* You don't really need the inventory for this one, since anyone with this gift could be identified blindfolded. These are people who in other life circumstances would have grown up to be General Patton or Turkish prison guards. In churches that are truly gift-based, the wedding hostess actually functions as senior pastor.

*(continued)*

6. *Kitchen Hostess.* This is to wedding hostess what minor leagues are to the majors: a place where promising rookies can get experience and fading veterans can enjoy a last fling at playing the game before it's time to hang up the spikes.

7. *Helping People Discover Their Spiritual Gifts.*

—John Ortberg
*(Recruiting, Training)*

Dates used:_____

—Dik LaPine
*(Perception, Relationships)*

Dates used:_____

221

—Dik LaPine
*(Attitude, Relationships)*

Dates used:_____

# Theology

Here is a valuable tool to help with your congregation, board, even your peers. When in need of additional class or clout, simply select any three-digit number at random. Instantly you have the words to impress and inspire.

For example, a "567" would be an "Ingenuous theoretical gratuity." Such verbosity can go a long way toward substantiating your position on anything—especially since no one would dare admit he didn't understand what you said.

| | | |
|---|---|---|
| 0 Veracious | 0 Ecclesiastical | 0 Tenet |
| 1 Reverential | 1 Canonical | 1 Doctrine |
| 2 Integrated | 2 Theological | 2 Concept |
| 3 Preferential | 3 Spiritual | 3 Assurance |
| 4 Consecrated | 4 Intangible | 4 Credence |
| 5 Ingenuous | 5 Incorporeal | 5 Speculation |
| 6 Comparable | 6 Theoretical | 6 Dogma |
| 7 Systematized | 7 Patristic | 7 Gratuity |
| 8 Balanced | 8 Sacerdotal | 8 Piety |
| 9 Transitional | 9 Ecumenical | 9 Perception |

—Boyce Mouton
*(Egotism, Intimidation)*

Dates used:_____

# Index

**Bold face** indicates major headings
and the pages on which they're found.

**Abstinence** . . . . . . . . . .**7**

Abundant Life . . . . . . . .87

**Acceptance** . . . . . . . . . .**7**

Accidents . . . . . . . . . . .9

Addictions . . . . . . . . . .163

Admiration . . . . . . . . . .108

**Adultery** . . . . . . . . . . .**8,** 167, 168

**Advent** . . . . . . . . . . . .**8**

**Afflictions** . . . . . . . . . .**9, 10,** 125

Age . . . . . . . . . . . . . . .**8,** 42

**Aging** . . . . . . . . . . . . .**11, 12,** 13, 121, 152, 185

Alcohol . . . . . . . . . . . . .168

Anonymity . . . . . . . . . .151

Anxiety . . . . . . . . . . . . .9, 10

Appearance . . . . . . . . . .137

**Appearances** . . . . . . . . .**13,** 67

Arguing . . . . . . . . . . . .112

Arguments . . . . . . . . . .146

Assimilation . . . . . . . . .158

**Assumptions** . . . . . . . . .7, **14**

Atonement . . . . . . . . . .144

**Attitude** . . . . . . . . . . . .9, 11, **15, 16,** 43, 86, 152, 222

**Authenticity** . . . . . . . . .**17**

Backbiting . . . . . . . . . .48

**Bad Days** . . . . . . . . . . .**194, 195, 196, 197**

**Baptism** . . . . . . . . . . . .**19, 20,** 97

Beauty . . . . . . . . . . . . .76, 189

Belief . . . . . . . . . . . . . . .69

**Beliefs** . . . . . . . . . . . . .**21**

**Bible** . . . . . . . . . . . . .**22, 23,** 54, 86

Bills . . . . . . . . . . . . . .32

**Blame** . . . . . . . . . . . . .**24, 25, 26**

Boards . . . . . . . . . . . . .28, 36, 97, 180

**Body of Christ** . . . . . . . .**27**

Bondage . . . . . . . . . . . .218

Boredom . . . . . . . . . . . .136

**Budgets** . . . . . . . . . . . . .**27**

**Bureaucracy** . . . . . . . . .**28**

Busyness . . . . . . . . . . . .119

Calm . . . . . . . . . . . . . .118

Certainty . . . . . . . . . . . .122

Character . . . . . . . . . . .13

Chastity . . . . . . . . . . . .7

Children . . . . . . . . . . . .53, 76, 111, 126, 127

Christ's Suffering . . . . . . .49

Choirs . . . . . . . . . . . . . .187

**Christmas** . . . . . . . . . .8, **29,** 143

**Church** . . . . . . . . . . . .21, 27, **29, 30,** 114, 158, 170, 196, 200, 201, 202, 204, 206

**Church and State** . . . . . .**31**

**Church Planting** . . . . . .**198**

**Church Talk** . . . . . . . . .**200, 201**

**Cleverness** . . . . . . . . . .**32**

College . . . . . . . . . . . . .78

**Comfort** . . . . . . . . . . . .**33**

**Commitment** . . . . . . . . .**34,** 111, 149, 184

**Committees** . . . . . . . . .28, **35,** 82, 131

**Communication** . . . . . .27, 30, **36, 37, 38, 39,** 42, 115, 181

**Communion** . . . . . . . . .**40, 41, 42**

**Community** . . . . . . . . .**42,** 170

Comparison . . . . . . . . .89

**Compassion** . . . . . . . . .33, **43, 44,** 62, 85, 100

**Competition** . . . . . . . . .**45**

Complaining . . . . . . . . .16, 25, 54

Compliments . . . . . . . . .88, 169

**Computers** . . . . . . . . . .**202**

Confession . . . . . . . . . .72

Conflict . . . . . . . . . . . . .213

Confusion . . . . . . . . . . .20, 26, 35, 140, 201

Contentment . . . . . . . . .64, 96, 99, 128

Cooperation . . . . . . . . .61

**Counseling** . . . . . . . . . .**46,** 129, 151, **203**

Courage . . . . . . . . . . . .150

**Courtesy** . . . . . . . . . . .**47**

Covetousness . . . . . . . .81

**Creation** . . . . . . . . . . . .**47,** 59

**Crisis** . . . . . . . . . . . . . .**48**

**Criticism** . . . . . . . . . . .**48, 49,** 95, 101, 165, 166

Cross-Cultural Ministry . .116

**Crucifixion** . . . . . . . . .**49**

Culture . . . . . . . . . . . . .79

Curiosity . . . . . . . . . . . .175

Danger . . . . . . . . . . . . .14

Dating . . . . . . . . . . . . .189

**Death** . . . . . . . . . . . . .12, **51, 52,** 118

Debt . . . . . . . . . . . . . .27

Deceit . . . . . . . . . . . . .17

**Decision-making** . . . . . .**53**

Dedication . . . . . . . . . .44, 132

**Definitions** . . . . . . . . . .**204, 206**

Delay . . . . . . . . . . . . .129

**Delegation** . . . . . . . . . .**53**

Denominations . . . . . . .19

Dependence . . . . . . . . .98

Depression . . . . . . . . . .162

**Devotions** . . . . . . . . . . .**54**

Diet . . . . . . . . . . . . . .106, 107

Diplomacy . . . . . . . . . .165, 166

**Disappointment** . . . . . .**54,** 210

Discernment . . . . . . . . .200, 204, 206

**Discipleship** . . . . . . . . .54, **55**

Discipline . . . . . . . . . . .106, 107, 132

Disclosure . . . . . . . . . .217

Discouragement . . . . . .194, 195

**Discretion** . . . . . . . . . .**56**

Disharmony . . . . . . . . .112

Dishonesty . . . . . . . . . .90

Disobedience . . . . . . . .155

Distortion . . . . . . . . . .94

Divorce . . . . . . . . . . . .112

**Doubt** . . . . . . . . . . . . . .**57,** 70

**Easter** . . . . . . . . . . . . . .49, **59,** 82

Eavesdropping . . . . . . . . .135

Economy . . . . . . . . . . . .185

Egotism . . . . . . . . . . . . .223

Embarrassment . . . . . . . .91, 93, 186, 214

Emergencies . . . . . . . . . .48

**Employers** . . . . . . . . . . .**60, 61**

End Times . . . . . . . . . . . .140

Enthusiasm . . . . . . . . . . .180

Eternity . . . . . . . . . . . . .52

**Evangelism** . . . . . . . . . .39, 55, **62, 63, 64, 65, 66,** 96, 118

Evolution . . . . . . . . . . . .47

**Example** . . . . . . . . . . . .41, **67,** 71, 161

Excuses . . . . . . . . . . . . .34, 120, 185

**Exercise** . . . . . . . . . . . .**208**

Expectations . . . . . . . . .32, 40, 86, 87, 99, 115, 123, 148, 160, 215

Extravagance . . . . . . . . . .171

Fairness . . . . . . . . . . . . .51

Faith . . . . . . . . . . . . . . .21**, 69, 70,** 134

Family . . . . . . . . . . . . . .88, 154

Fat . . . . . . . . . . . . . . . . .150

**Fatherhood** . . . . . . . . . .**71,** 77

Fathers . . . . . . . . . . . . . .76

Favor . . . . . . . . . . . . . . .81

Fear . . . . . . . . . . . . . . . .14, 118, 173

Fellowship . . . . . . . . . . .19, 29, 114, 156, 157

Fitness . . . . . . . . . . . . . .184
Foresight . . . . . . . . . . . .160
**Forgiveness** . . . . . . . . .**71, 72,** 155
**Free Will** . . . . . . . . . . .**73**
Friendship . . . . . . . . . .121, 156, 157
**Frugality** . . . . . . . . . . .**73**
**Fruit of the Spirit** . . . . . .**74**
Frustration . . . . . . . . . .60
Funerals . . . . . . . . . . . .12, 197
Future . . . . . . . . . . . . .139, 140
Generosity . . . . . . . . . .160, 172
Gifts . . . . . . . . . . . . . .29
**Giving** . . . . . . . . . . . .40, **75,** 148, 154, 171
God . . . . . . . . . . . . . .103
**God's Call** . . . . . . . . . .**75**
God's Direction . . . . . . .73
God's Gift . . . . . . . . . . .19
**God's Image** . . . . . . . . .**76**
**God's Love** . . . . . . . . . .**76, 77**
**God's Omniscience** . . . . .**78,** 175
**God's Wrath** . . . . . . . . .**79, 80**
Godlessness . . . . . . . . .79
**Good News** . . . . . . . . . .**210**
Gossip . . . . . . . . . . . . .48
**Grace** . . . . . . . . . . . . .77, **81**
Grandparents . . . . . . . .137
**Greed** . . . . . . . . . . . . .43, 78, **81**
**Growth** . . . . . . . . . . . .**82**

**Guest Speakers** . . . . . . **209**
**Guilt** . . . . . . . . . . . . . .24, 46, 47, **83**
Happiness . . . . . . . . . . .99, 183
**Hardheartedness** . . . . . **85,** 203
Hardships . . . . . . . . . . .128
Harmony . . . . . . . . . . .37
**Health** . . . . . . . . . . . . . .**86,** 133, 176, 184
**Heaven** . . . . . . . . . . . .75, **86, 87**
Help . . . . . . . . . . . . . . .38
Helpfulness . . . . . . . . . .85
Heritage . . . . . . . . . . . .137
Heroes . . . . . . . . . . . . .71
Holy Spirit . . . . . . . . . .142
**Home** . . . . . . . . . . . . . .**88**
**Honesty** . . . . . . . . . . . .65, 71, **88, 89, 90,** 93, 185, 215
Hope . . . . . . . . . . . . . .123
**Humility** . . . . . . . . . . .88, **91, 93, 94,** 137, 198
Idols . . . . . . . . . . . . . . .186
**Illustrations** . . . . . . . . .**212**
Impact . . . . . . . . . . . . .31
**Impatience** . . . . . . . . . .**95**
Impressions . . . . . . . . .209
**Inadequacy** . . . . . . . . .**96**
**Incarnation** . . . . . . . . .**96**
Incrimination . . . . . . . .83
Indictment . . . . . . . . . .83
Inerrancy . . . . . . . . . . .22, 57
Inferiority . . . . . . . . . . .96

Influence . . . . . . . . . . . .53, 56

**Innovation** . . . . . . . . . .**97**

Insecurity . . . . . . . . . . . .189

**Insensitivity** . . . . . . . . .**98**

Insight . . . . . . . . . . . . . .170

Integrity . . . . . . . . . . . . .65, 100

Intercession . . . . . . . . . .135

Intimacy . . . . . . . . . . . . .103

Intimidation . . . . . . . . . .223

**Jobs** . . . . . . . . . . . . . . .**99, 100**

Jokes . . . . . . . . . . . . . .212

Judging . . . . . . . . . . . . .49

**Judging Others** . . . . . . .**100, 101**

**Knowing God** . . . . . . . .**103**

Last Supper . . . . . . . . . .42

**Last Words** . . . . . . . . . .**213**

Laughter . . . . . . . . . . . .37

Laziness . . . . . . . . . . . .12

**Leadership** . . . . . . . . . .**105,** 133, 179, 213

**Legalism** . . . . . . . . . . .**106, 107**

Lifestyle . . . . . . . . . . . .161

Listening . . . . . . . . . . . .38, 181

**Love** . . . . . . . . . . . . . . .71, 88, **108, 109**

Lying . . . . . . . . . . . . . .90, 129

Manners . . . . . . . . . . . .116

**Marriage** . . . . . . . . . . .44, 45, 98, 108, **111, 112,** 126, 127,
     141, 145, 149, 153, 154, 177, 183, 184

Materialism . . . . . . . . . .66

**Men and Women** . . . . . .**113**

**Men's Ministry** . . . . . . .**114**

Mercy . . . . . . . . . . . . . .16

**Ministry** . . . . . . . . . . . .**115,** 117, 133, 208

Miracles . . . . . . . . . . . .57

Miserliness . . . . . . . . . .75

**Missions** . . . . . . . . . . .62, 65, 75, 96, 105, **116, 117, 118**

Mistakes . . . . . . . . . . . .179, 194, 195, 197

Misunderstanding . . . . . .39

Money . . . . . . . . . . . . .27, 73, 145

**Mortality** . . . . . . . . . . .52, **118**

**Motherhood** . . . . . . . . .47, **119**

Murder . . . . . . . . . . . . .167

Music . . . . . . . . . . . . . .65, 113

**Musicians** . . . . . . . . . .**120**

Neglect . . . . . . . . . . . . .141

**Neighbors** . . . . . . . . . .**121**

**New Year's Day** . . . . . .**122**

Obligation . . . . . . . . . . .218

**Optimism** . . . . . . . . . .86, **123**

**Panic** . . . . . . . . . . . . .**125**

**Parenting** . . . . . . . . . . .53, 80, 111, **126, 127, 128**

Parents . . . . . . . . . . . . .167

**Pastoral Care** . . . . . . . .**129,** 203, 208, 214

**Patience** . . . . . . . . . . . .95, **129,** 136

Peace . . . . . . . . . . . . . .8

**Peacemaking** . . . . . . . .**130**

**Peer Pressure** . . . . . . . .11, **131**

Perception . . . . . . . . . . .221

**Perseverance** . . . . . . . .**132, 133**

Perspective . . . . . . . . . .20, 51, 101, 210, 217

Persuasion . . . . . . . . . .80

Pessimism . . . . . . . . . . .70

Plans . . . . . . . . . . . . . .54

Politics . . . . . . . . . . . . .31

**Popularity** . . . . . . . . . .**133**

Praise . . . . . . . . . . . . . .169

**Prayer** . . . . . . . . . . . . .41, 73, 76, **134, 135, 136, 214**

**Preachers** . . . . . . . . . . .**137**

Preaching . . . . . . . . . . .209

Predictions . . . . . . . . . .139

Prejudice . . . . . . . . . . . .7

Pretense . . . . . . . . . . . .191

**Pride** . . . . . . . . . . . . . .17, 45, 91, 113, **137, 138,** 150

Priorities . . . . . . . . . . . .66, 171

Privacy . . . . . . . . . . . . .46

Procrastination . . . . . . .36, 129

Profanity . . . . . . . . . . . .47

**Prophecy** . . . . . . . . . . .122, **139, 140**

**Pulpit Committees** . . . . .**215**

**Punishment** . . . . . . . . .**140**

Purity . . . . . . . . . . . . . .7

Rebellion . . . . . . . . . . .15

Recognition . . . . . . . . . .133

Recruiting . . . . . . . . . . .63, 219

Recycling . . . . . . . . . . .29

**Relationships** . . . . . . . .**141,** 146, 221, 222

Reminiscence . . . . . . . .128

**Renewal** . . . . . . . . . . . .**142, 143**

**Repentance** . . . . . . . . .72, **144,** 155

**Resourcefulness** . . . . . .**145**

Respect . . . . . . . . . . . . .130

Responsibility . . . . . . . .24, 25, 26, 55, 134, 145

Rest . . . . . . . . . . . . . .147

**Resumes** . . . . . . . . . . .**217**

Resurrection . . . . . . . . .59

**Retirement** . . . . . . . . . .**145**

**Revenge** . . . . . . . . . . . .**146**

Revival . . . . . . . . . . . . .142, 143

Rewards . . . . . . . . . . . .135

Rights . . . . . . . . . . . . . .183

Role Models . . . . . . . . .67

Romance . . . . . . . . . . . .108

**Sabbath** . . . . . . . . . . . .**147**

**Sacrifice** . . . . . . . . . . . .41, **148, 149,** 171

Salvation . . . . . . . . . . . .19, 163

Sanctification . . . . . . . .20

Savings . . . . . . . . . . . . .73

**Scripture** . . . . . . . . . . .**150**

Self-control . . . . . . . . . .74

**Self-esteem** . . . . . . . . .**150, 151**

Self-reliance . . . . . . . . .113

Selfishness . . . . . . . . . .81

Sense of Humor . . . . . . .11

# Index

# Index

**Servanthood**  . . . . . . . . .138, **152**

**Service**  . . . . . . . . . . . . .**218**

**Sharing**  . . . . . . . . . . . .33, **153, 154**

Silence  . . . . . . . . . . . . .130

**Sin**  . . . . . . . . . . . . . . . .20, 25, 49, 56, 100, 144, **155,** 168

Singing  . . . . . . . . . . . . .120

Single Adults  . . . . . . . . .12

Small Church  . . . . . . . .198

**Small Groups**  . . . . . . . .131, **156, 157**

Smugness  . . . . . . . . . . .150

Spiritual Blindness  . . . . .94

**Spiritual Gifts**  . . . . . . .**219**

**Sports**  . . . . . . . . . . . . .35, **158**

**Staff Relations**  . . . . . . .105, **221, 222**

Stealing  . . . . . . . . . . . .100

**Stewardship**  . . . . . . . . .75, **160**

Stinginess  . . . . . . . . . . .42, 160

Stories  . . . . . . . . . . . . .212

**Stress**  . . . . . . . . . . . . . .10, 111, **160, 161, 162,** 176

Sunday School  . . . . . . .22, 140, 167

**Support Group**  . . . . . . .**163**

**Tactfulness**  . . . . . . . . .**165, 166**

Taxes  . . . . . . . . . . . . . .172

Teamwork  . . . . . . . . . . .48

Technology  . . . . . . . . . .202

Teenagers  . . . . . . . . . . .128

Television  . . . . . . . . . . .74

Temptation  . . . . . . . . . .89

**Ten Commandments** . . .8, 15, **167, 168, 169**

**Thankfulness** . . . . . . . . .**170**

**Theology** . . . . . . . . . . .**170, 223**

**Thrift** . . . . . . . . . . . . . .**171**

Tidiness . . . . . . . . . . . .119

**Tithing** . . . . . . . . . . . . .**171, 172**

Training . . . . . . . . . . . .219

Travel . . . . . . . . . . . . . .117, 173

Trials . . . . . . . . . . . . . .125, 162, 196

Trouble . . . . . . . . . . . . .9, 10

**Trust** . . . . . . . . . . . . . .69, **173**

**Uncertainty** . . . . . . . . .**175**

Understanding . . . . . . . .170

**Unhappiness** . . . . . . . .**176**

**Unity** . . . . . . . . . . . . . .**177**

**Ushers** . . . . . . . . . . . . .138, 141, **178,** 187

Valentine's Day . . . . . . .108

Vanity . . . . . . . . . . . . . .189

Violence . . . . . . . . . . . .35

**Vision** . . . . . . . . . . . . .35, **179, 180**

Visitation . . . . . . . . . . .34

Visitors . . . . . . . . . . . . .29

**Volunteers** . . . . . . . . . .30, 178, **181**

**Weddings** . . . . . . . . . . .112, 141, 153, 177, **183, 184**

**Weight** . . . . . . . . . . . . .**184**

Wisdom . . . . . . . . . . . .61

Witnessing . . . . . . . . . .63

Women . . . . . . . . . . . . .155

## Index

**Work** . . . . . . . . . . . . . . .60, 99, 145, **185**

Workplace . . . . . . . . . . .53, 191

Works . . . . . . . . . . . . . .81

Worldliness . . . . . . . . . .64

**Worry** . . . . . . . . . . . . . .**185**

**Worship** . . . . . . . . . . . .113, 147, 154, 178, **186, 187**

**Youth** . . . . . . . . . . . . . .**189**

**Zeal** . . . . . . . . . . . . . . .**191**